Empowering Teachers

*To my brother, Gregory, who has devoted
his life to children with special needs.*

Joseph

To my father, and in memory of Mom.

Jo

Empowering Teachers

What Successful Principals Do

Joseph Blase
Jo Roberts Blase

CORWIN PRESS, INC.
A Sage Publications Company
Thousand Oaks, California

For information address:

Corwin Press, Inc.
2455 Teller Road
Thousand Oaks, California 91320

SAGE Publications Ltd.
6 Bonhill Street
London EC2A 4PU
United Kingdom

SAGE Publications India Pvt. Ltd.
M-32 Market
Greater Kailash I
New Delhi 110 048 India

Printed in the United States of America

Library of Congress Cataloging-in-Publication Data

Blase, Joseph.
    Empowering teachers : what successful principals do / Joseph
Blase, Jo Roberts Blase.
    Includes Bibliographical references and index.
    ISBN 0-8039-6091-3 (alk. paper). — ISBN 0-8039-6092-1 (pbk.
alk. paper)
    1. Teacher participation in administration—United States.
2. School principals—United States. 3. Teacher-principal
relationships. I. Blase, Jo Roberts. II. Title.
LB2806.45.B53 1994
371.2'012—dc20   94-30531

This book is printed on acid-free paper that meets Environmental Protection Agency standards for recycled paper.

94 95 96 97 98 10 9 8 7 6 5 4 3 2 1

Corwin Press Production Editor: Diane S. Foster

Contents

Foreword

Empowering Teachers: What Successful Principals Do is a book greatly
needed in our profession. It speaks from the minds and hearts of
teachers about the practices of their principals that allow them to
make extraordinary efforts on behalf of students. These teachers work
at all levels and in urban, rural, and suburban areas. What they have
in common is membership in purposeful school communities that
are trying to realize the essence of public education in a democracy.

As a principal in one of these schools, after four years of shared
governance, said, "It's really hard to explain. You'd almost have to
live it day-to-day to really sense the excitement, the difference that
it is making." What this principal was speaking about was the complex
and positive changes in self, faculty, parents, and, most important,
students. The exhilarations, anxieties, and, at times, frustrations are
all part of refocusing the principalship from a hierarchical, line-
authority position to embodying the collective democratic will of
the school.

Professors Blase and Blase explain in a clear, comprehensive, and friendly manner what these successful principals do—their behaviors, their attitudes, and their practices. Blase and Blase write directly to aspiring and present principals who believe in the wisdom, care, and commitment of faculty to make difficult decisions together about good education for all students. These principals do not see the equal sharing of authority as a threat but simply as the best way for a school to practice moral authority for education in a democratic society.

This book will be a thoughtful friend for all those readers who travel down the road of providing a just and powerful education for all. As the old African proverb states, "It takes an entire village to raise a child." In these schools, it takes an entire school community to truly educate all students.

At the time of the study, the 11 schools reported on were in their third year of shared governance implementation. Each year since, they have become bolder in vision and practice. These schools have made consistent educational advancements for students and have increased involvement of parents and community members. They have garnered recognitions and awards and been featured on national television shows and in magazine reports and newspaper stories. But these schools are no different from most others in terms of limited resources, political pressures, and the unpredictable day-to-day events that occur in the busy life of schools. The real difference is that in these schools principals and teachers continue to believe in each other and their professional ideals.

Read this book, keep it by your side, and let it be a guide to your own work.

Carl D. Glickman
Professor, Department of Educational Leadership
Chair, Program for School Improvement
University of Georgia

Foreword

What do frogs, crabs, and President Clinton have to do with shared governance at Pinckneyville Middle School in Gwinnett County, Georgia? Since becoming a charter school in the shared governance organization of the League of Professional Schools, our Leadership Council has taken two summer retreats, one at a south Georgia farm and one at a beach house in Florida. Our resulting shared governance process contributed to our award, presented by the President in May 1993, of a National Blue Ribbon School.

Six years ago Judi Rogers and I came to Pinckneyville as the school's two new administrators. Previously there had been discord between the PTA and the school administration. There were also factions within the faculty because many had felt the sting of the community and school problems. Concurrent with the change in leadership were also many changes in personnel; however, the distrust seemed entrenched.

During that first year many new programs were started. There were several attempts to bring about communication between the community and the faculty and to heal the painful wounds. Soon, members of the community responded, and parents and teachers began working together harmoniously. But the divisions within the faculty remained, and widespread suspicion and fear were fueled by wholesale gossip. Repeated attempts to involve faculty in decisions and policymaking were frustrating and seemed futile. What could we do? Eventually, a small group of teachers and leaders suggested that we needed to find another vehicle to bring the faculty together. Thus began our search for such a catalyst.

In January 1990, Judi and I and two teachers attended a 2-day League of Professional Schools workshop. We had no idea that this would provide the seed for the growth we desired. As the workshop progressed, we came to understand the premises and the significance of the shared governance restructuring effort, and we realized that this model was exactly what we needed.

A week later, we carried out our plan to introduce shared governance at our faculty meeting. For the sake of contrasting this approach with that of traditional staff development plans, we began with a little joke: We told the faculty that we had just attended a conference on school improvement and that we would hold a **mandatory** workshop for all faculty members on the following weekend to share what we had learned and how it would be implemented in our school! Needless to say, the faculty members were not pleased at the prospect of having ideas imposed on them—what professionals wouldn't be offended at this? We used this response as a platform to discuss shared decision making, shared governance, liaison groups, and the functions of an Executive Council. *As a result, the faculty unanimously voted to become a League member.* Then, we randomly broke the faculty and staff into six liaison groups, and each group elected an Executive Council representative. After a *1-hour* faculty meeting, we had begun our involvement in shared governance.

Our initial efforts ranged in focus from the broad purposes of our work to the minutiae of expectations for individuals in the role of liaison group member. As assumptions and parameters were clarified, a basic understanding was built. Ultimately, this simple first step became the foundation of *trust* necessary for further growth.

Within 2 years our shared decision-making efforts had expanded to the point that our Leadership Council became overloaded. We decided to retreat to a south Georgia farm to spend some uninterrupted time thinking, talking, and making decisions about our functioning. We made good decisions and we had fun! Teachers caught some of the farm's plentiful frogs and (gently, of course) placed them in the most unusual places to be found by unsuspecting colleagues! The following summer we went to a teacher's beach house in Florida, and hermit crabs were the source of amusement during this retreat.

As I look back on the past 6 years, it is hard for me to believe that this is the same group. Yet I am reminded of our remarkable progress every day when I see the picture on my desk of President Clinton awarding me (our school) the National Blue Ribbon School Award for Excellence in 1993. For many of us, this is the external symbol of something we all know: that our venture into shared governance is wildly successful.

How does our exciting and effective shared governance project relate to this book? Well, I only wish we had this book 6 years ago! It could have saved us some anguish and doubt about what we were attempting to do. We have had to learn—the hard way—many of the points summarized and explained in this book. As demonstrated here *in the words of teachers*, shared governance is challenging, motivating, stressful, time-consuming, and rewarding. It is about working more effectively in groups, dealing with conflict, and seeing the big picture of school reform. Shared governance is *necessary* for real school improvement.

The principals described in this book are called "extraordinary" by the authors. Perhaps ordinary people do extraordinary things in times of crisis. Six years ago, in our time of crisis, our administrators and our teachers realized that if we did not begin to restructure our school we would not be able to meet the changing demands of our various and increasingly diverse publics. We began to understand what parents and students already knew: that education takes place in the classroom and that the only real educational reform would also take place in the classroom. Therefore, the classroom expert, the teacher, would be the best person to determine what this restructuring should look like and how it should be implemented.

This book explains how principals come to act on this belief. It describes the assumptions and philosophy underlying shared governance as well as the specific behaviors of effective shared governance leaders. Most important, the suggestions in this book have been validated by teachers who have been involved in successful shared decision making. In this way, the tenets of teacher empowerment are determined by teachers. The summaries at the end of each chapter can be used as guidelines for educators becoming involved in shared governance or as a checkup for educators who have been involved in the process for years. (We are presently using these summaries in our Leadership Council meetings.)

Ideas for facilitating empowerment (see Chapter 2) and for supporting risk taking (see Chapter 7) can be lost or ignored unless we remind ourselves to focus on them. At Pinckneyville we are always trying to improve our approach to shared governance, with yearly revisions since we began; Chapter 3 presents models of shared governance that we will review as we revise our approach. The increased emphasis that staff development has had in our school since we began our shared decision making is astounding, and Chapter 4 will be especially helpful in staff development planning. As a principal I am particularly interested in the shared leadership characteristics of the principals described in Chapter 6 and the summary of strategies used by the principals presented in Chapter 10. I also found the guidelines for praise and rewards in Chapter 8 fascinating in regard to teachers' feelings; this will help me in my constant struggle to find ways to support teachers in the tremendously important work they do. Our Leadership Council is particularly eager to study the strategies for promoting autonomy and innovation among faculty members detailed in Chapter 5 and the problem-solving hints in Chapter 9.

We at Pinckneyville feel that we are on a mission, that **we have a cause beyond any one of us.** With this comes the realization that schooling must focus on what is learned more than on what is taught and that when learning is not occurring teaching **will have to be transformed.** At times we feel somewhat alone in our efforts to bring about real change. While we know that others have embarked on shared governance efforts, the amount of shared governance at our school may be greater than that of other schools at the moment. It is still difficult to find others with similar experiences who can help us reflect on our work. This book will serve as a companion in our work, and it will help us relate our experiences to other educators. I believe it will help you, too.

Cindy Loe
Principal
Pinckneyville Middle School
Norcross, Georgia

Preface

This book is written for practicing and prospective principals who want to empower teachers. It is about what successful principals do and the "transformative effects" that such principals have on teachers' work both in the classroom and in the school generally.

Current efforts in the United States to restructure schools emphasize new types of governance and teacher empowerment. As such, the efforts that promise to dominate education during the 1990s are fundamentally different from what has appeared before. And although the critical role of the school principal in restructuring is widely recognized among educational practitioners and scholars, there are few research-based accounts of what successful principals actually do to implement new governance structures to empower teachers and to improve education. In fact, there are no detailed pictures of the strategies that successful principals use to empower teachers and what being empowered actually means to teachers.

This book, we believe, will provide welcome relief to practicing and prospective principals searching for basic understandings and guidelines about the kind of leadership—what we call "facilitative-democratic leadership"—that requires principals to reflect critically on the fundamental differences between controlling teachers and empowering them.

Empowering Teachers: What Successful Principals Do is drawn from a study of highly successful principals of schools affiliated with Carl Glickman's League of Professional Schools. This study focused on understanding the characteristics of shared governance principals that directly and indirectly contribute to teachers' sense of empowerment. The book is based on data collected from teachers; it is, in other words, representative of teachers' perspectives. The research protocol encouraged teachers to express themselves freely, in their own words and in full detail, about their principals—in order to identify empowering characteristics of principals and exactly how such characteristics affected them.

In this book, we present descriptions of what successful principals actually do—from the teachers' point of view—that leads to such impacts as improved motivation, self-esteem, confidence, commitment, innovation, autonomy, and reflection. We also present for consideration relevant concepts, models, and strategies from the literature that should help practitioners "think through" their approach to implementing shared governance. We believe that principals will improve their chances of constructing meaningful ways of working with teachers if they reflect critically about their leadership using a knowledge base directly relevant to this challenge.

What does effective, facilitative, empowering leadership look like? What approaches to leadership produce the remarkable benefits identified with empowered teachers? This book is intended to provide some initial answers to these and other questions. Chapter 1 presents a brief overview of the professional literature on teacher empowerment and empowering leadership as well as a brief description of the study on which this book is based. Chapters 2 and 3 focus, respectively, on two fundamental principal strategies—building trust and developing enabling structures. In Chapter 4 we examine how principals use basic supportive resources such as staff development to enhance teachers' instructional capabilities. Two strategies—extending autonomy and encouraging innovation—are discussed in Chapter 5.

The effects of several personal characteristics of principals, including optimism, caring, honesty, friendliness, and enthusiasm, are highlighted in Chapter 6. Chapter 7 focuses on the significance of reducing risk and threat to teachers. The benefits of rewarding teachers are examined in Chapter 8, whereas in Chapter 9 the importance of a problem-solving orientation is discussed. Each chapter concludes with a discussion of several guidelines for the reader's consideration. Chapter 10, the final chapter, summarizes the findings and conclusions of the study, presents a portrait of today's successful shared governance principal, and discusses possibilities for the future of facilitative-democratic leadership in schools. Research methods and recommended books are found in Resources A and B, respectively.

This book is about exceptionally effective, even extraordinary school principals and how they are meeting the challenges for leadership in a new, exciting, and promising era of educational reform. It describes the major elements of successful facilitative leadership from the perspectives of the very people who experience and appear to thrive on such leadership. The book describes what can be expected when school principals trust and respect teachers not only as knowledgeable professionals in the classroom but also as willing, committed participants in transforming American education. It is about principals who understand that to improve American education both teachers and students must experience the school as a place that provides innovative and dynamic opportunities for growth and development. In *The Predictable Failure of Educational Reform* (Jossey-Bass, 1990), Seymour Sarason states,

> Whatever factors, variables, and ambience are conducive for the growth, development, and self-regard of a school's staff are precisely those that are crucial to obtaining the same consequences for students in a classroom. To focus on the latter and ignore or gloss over the former is an invitation to disillusionment. (p. 152)

Reference

Sarason, S. (1990). *The predictable failure of educational reform: Can we change the course before it's too late?* San Francisco: Jossey-Bass.

Acknowledgments

We wish to express our deep appreciation to the professors and practitioners who reviewed earlier drafts of this book and provided valuable feedback to us: Carl Glickman, Sherry Dungan, Jimmy Jordan, Peggy Kirby, Laura Lester, Cindy Loe, Barbara Lunsford, and Judi Rogers. Excellent technical support was provided by Donna Bell, Linda Edwards, Cheryl Smith, and Art Crawley.

As shared governance authors, we note that our contributions to the research project and the material herein are equal.

Joseph Blase
Jo Roberts Blase
University of Georgia

About the Authors

Joseph Blase is a professor of educational leadership at the University of Georgia. Since receiving his Ph.D. in 1980 from Syracuse University his research has focused entirely on understanding the work lives of teachers. He has published many studies in the areas of teacher stress, relations between teachers' personal and professional lives, teacher socialization, and principal-teacher relationships. His recent work, focused on school-level micropolitics, received the 1988 Davis Memorial Award given by the University Council for Educational Administration. Blase edited *The Politics of Life in Schools: Power, Conflict, and Cooperation* (1991) and coauthored, with Peggy Kirby, *Bringing Out the Best in Teachers: What Effective Principals Do* (1992). He is currently coauthoring a book about the micropolitics of school leadership.

Jo Roberts Blase is an associate professor of educational leadership at the University of Georgia and a former public school teacher, principal, and director of staff development. She received a Ph.D. in educational administration, curriculum, and supervision in 1983 from the University of Colorado at Boulder. Through work with the Beginning Principal Study National Research Team as well as with the Georgia League of Professional Schools (and educators with whom she consults), she has pursued her interest in the study of preparation and entry to educational leadership and instructional leadership as it relates to supervisory discourse. Winner of the 1983 American Association of School Administrators Outstanding Research Award, Blase has recently published articles in the *Journal of Staff Development*, the *Journal of Curriculum and Supervision*, and *Organization Theory Dialog*. She has also authored chapters in books on becoming a principal, school renewal, supervision, and organizational discourse and is currently coauthoring a book about principals' perspectives on democratic leadership.

Empowering schools must be educational communities coalesced around a core of values guided by a sense of hope and possibility, grounded in a belief in justice and democracy. These communities must nourish the voices of all their members; they must provide contexts in which people can speak and listen, learn and grow, and let go of ideas in order to move on to better ideas. Such learning communities must create climates in which all members are respected and listened to. They must be places in which teachers (but not only teachers) have a voice in decision making and the ongoing impetus to look at themselves, their schools, and their world critically. In order to do this, the nature of power in schools must be transformed, the hierarchy of decision making must be transformed, the structure of the school day must be transformed, and the way we interact with colleagues and students must be radically reexamined.

—Seth Kreisberg,
Transforming Power: Domination,
Empowerment, and Education (1992), p. 151

1

Sharing Governance

... the empowerment of teachers has more to do with individual deportment than with the ability to boss others. This is not the strutting, order-issuing sort of empowerment. Rather, it is the ability to exercise one's craft with quiet confidence and to help shape the way the job is done. Empowerment becomes inevitable when teachers have so much to offer and are so sure about what they know that they can no longer be shut out of the policy-making process.

—Maeroff (1988), p. 475

In recent years, the role of the principal has come to be seen as critical in implementing shared decision making (Malen & Ogawa, 1988). Central to this approach are the development of cooperative relationships in order to reach collaboratively agreed-on goals (Dunlap & Goldman, 1991), the recognition of teachers' educational expertise (Maeroff, 1988), the leader's "power with" as opposed to "power over" orientation (Kreisberg, 1992), and the primacy of an instructional focus (Glickman, 1993).

However, empirical research provides few detailed pictures of the day-to-day dynamics of sharing governance of a school with empowered teachers. Absent in particular from the reported research are teachers' perspectives on the performance of successful facilitative leaders as well as the effects of that performance. Many other areas also need to be illuminated: organization, communication, and procedures in shared governance schools; the quality and degree of teacher involvement; the characteristics of successful principals in such schools; and the results of sharing authority with teachers and encouraging them to exercise control of their professional environment (see, e.g., Osterman, 1989).

The need for more *field-based* studies of the dynamics of shared decision making and shared governance in schools has been recognized (Conley, 1991). This book addresses that need by expanding the knowledge base regarding how successful shared governance principals work to empower teachers and by describing the reported effects that these leaders have on teachers' sense of empowerment.

Teacher Empowerment

Current conceptions of teacher empowerment cover a wide range of ideas, including the following:

- Teacher involvement in school governance
- Granting new respect to teachers and improving their work conditions
- Higher salaries and new professional structures
- Teacher revolution to gain control of the profession
- Increasing teacher autonomy and professionalism

(Readers are referred to Carnegie Forum, 1986; Maeroff, 1988; Spring, 1988.)

Bolin's (1989) definition, which encompasses all of the concepts noted above, is that teacher empowerment requires "investing in teachers the right to participate in the determination of school goals and policies and the right to exercise professional judgment about the content of the curriculum and means of instruction" (p. 83). This definition assumes that teaching is fundamentally a *moral* (or value-based) activity, and as such, it requires that teachers have *expertise* to engage in thoughtful deliberations and *professional authority* to participate meaningfully in decisions about their schools and classrooms. Principals who embrace these concepts rather than merely expecting teachers to implement other people's visions for schools will accord teachers respect and dignity and will help them to be more fully responsible for work-related decisions. *This combination of respect and dignity is the essence of empowerment.*

Finally, an important aspect of empowerment is that it is a *democratic value*, and "teachers should, as concerned citizens, as protectors of the truth, and as participants in the schooling enterprise, be allowed to voice their opinions about educational policy" (Tate, 1991, p. 5). *Democratic empowerment* through shared governance—including involvement of staff, parents, *and students*—lies at the heart of successful principals' practice.

What Does Teacher Empowerment Look Like?

Using evidence from teacher narratives and 9 months of on-site daily observations in a school of 40 empowered teachers, Melenyzer (1990) sought to discover what teacher empowerment means to teachers and how empowerment is accomplished. From the teachers' data, Melenyzer constructed this definition of empowerment:

> The opportunity and confidence to act upon one's ideas and to influence the way one performs in one's profession. True empowerment leads to increased professionalism as teachers assume responsibility for and an involvement in the decision making process. (p. 16)

Melenyzer found that the meanings and social actions that teachers associated with empowerment are consistent with the ideals espoused by teachers' associations and with the principles of conservative and liberal educational theorists. She also found teacher empowerment to be consistent with the ideals of "transformative leadership." In this form of leadership, others are given responsibility, and their potential is released to make their actions and decisions count (Sergiovanni, 1989). When Melenyzer (1990) compared her findings with models of empowerment discussed in the educational literature, she found that the empowered teachers in her study were not "able to transform the social order in the interests of social justice, equality, and the development of a social democracy" (McLaren, 1988, p. 3). Melenyzer (1990) concluded that empowered teachers have only a limited "political" vision and, in practice, rarely seek to be emancipated from institutional and societal constraints on their work.

The Impetus for Teacher Empowerment

In the 1980s, *A Nation at Risk* (National Commission on Excellence in Education, 1983), an extensive study of American schools commissioned by the U.S. Department of Education, ushered in a national educational reform movement, and numerous reports (see, e.g., Carnegie Forum, 1986; Education Commission of the States, 1986; Holmes Group Executive Board, 1986; Wise, 1986) and high-impact books such as Boyer's (1983) *High School,* Goodlad's (1984) *A Place Called School,* and Sizer's (1984) *Horace's Compromise* called for massive changes to help schools achieve educational excellence. But by the end of the decade, Glickman (1989) and others popularized the view that teachers should be considered part of the *solution* to educational problems, not the source of such problems. This idea is central to the second reform wave that now emphasizes teacher *empowerment,* active *involvement of teachers in decision making,* and *shared governance*— that is, control of and influence by teachers over events affecting teachers themselves.

In addition, Melenyzer (1990) has argued that the critical emancipatory perspective (Apple, 1982; Cherryholmes, 1988; Freire, 1985; Giroux & McLaren, 1986) also promotes a strong concern for teacher empowerment. According to this perspective, teachers are expected to confront "oppressive" societal forces through reflective political action. By comparison, the liberal view of teacher empowerment (which, incidentally, does not address broad societal conditions), subscribed to by writers such as Glickman (1989) and Lightfoot (1986), emphasizes the capacity of empowered teachers to improve conditions *in their classrooms*. Finally, the conservative view (e.g., Lieberman, 1988; Maeroff, 1988) equates empowerment with professionalism; teachers are given new respect through the recognition and improvement of their work conditions.

The National Education Association, the American Federation of Teachers, and the United Federation of Teachers have also supported empowerment as local, state, and national goals. In fact, increased professionalization of teaching and restructuring schools for teacher empowerment have become the watchwords of the 1990s. Educational leaders are being asked to surrender power and to share power *with* rather than holding power *over* teachers in the belief that this power sharing will release the great potential of teachers to effect the improvement of schools and student achievement.

Empowering Leadership

Barth (1988) noted that a principal's most important challenge is one of *tapping teachers' expertise and experience* to facilitate enlightened decisions and build better educational programs. Yet we currently have little insight into which factors are crucial to shared decision making in schools. Until this study, the specifics of how to implement shared governance had been largely uninvestigated (Immegart, 1988; Simpson, 1989).

The professional literature suggests that failures (or mixed successes) in initiating active teacher involvement in decision making may result, in part, because principals lack the particular leadership skills (Goodlad, 1984) and basic knowledge essential to planning and change in shared governance operations (Carman, 1987; Gladder, 1990; Little, 1986). Our study data demonstrate that teacher empowerment, shared governance, or participative decision making—governance forms that have teacher decision making at their core—require, at minimum, educational leaders who consider their school's readiness, their personal philosophy, and their leadership behavior. We found that the behavior of successful shared governance principals takes each of these three factors into consideration.

Fundamental Considerations

Readiness

In his study of school restructuring, Bredeson (1989) described readiness as an important antecedent to empowerment; teachers who were unprepared for participation in decision making were described as "curious individuals cautiously peering into 'the cave' to see what was there" (p. 18). Bredeson's work suggests that, depending on career and adult stage of development, teachers have varying levels of engagement and commitment to team efforts and governance issues. Shared governance principals recognized these readiness factors and also seemed to understand what conditions foster self-governance. In one of Bredeson's study sites, an ever expanding network of trained professionals worked regularly on problem-solving teams. At another site, in contrast, empowerment was seen by teachers as "an invitation" to professionalism. In both cases, the messages of empowerment were reflected in professional behaviors and daily worklife patterns and relationships. (Readiness is further discussed in Chapter 3.)

A Participatory Leadership Philosophy

Principals who believe that the knowledge, work, and decisions related to students are (or should be) substantially under teacher control adhere to a democratic shared governance orientation. Such principals are not benevolent dictators, falsely involving teachers in empty decisions that have little or no influence on school operations, nor are they authoritarian bosses, co-opting the professionals they view as mere subordinates. Rather, they hold the following beliefs (see Conley, 1988, pp. 7-10):

1. *The primary control of pedagogical knowledge should be left to teachers.* This is the belief that professional teachers *create* pedagogical knowledge and that they continuously refine and adapt their knowledge.
2. *Teaching activities are nonroutine.* This is the belief that teaching activities are variable and constantly changing, thus *re-*

quiring innovation and experimentation to counter meaningless standardization.

3. *The teacher's primary work activity is decision making.* This is the belief that teachers make decisions in highly *unpredictable and interactive* situations, requiring sophisticated and creative solutions.

Leadership Behaviors

Our findings about successful shared governance principals generally agree with the few studies that have investigated leadership strategies and their impacts on teacher empowerment. For example, Reitzug (1994) conceptualized three major categories of principal behavior (support, facilitation, and revealing possibilities) that contribute to teacher empowerment. Other descriptions of teacher advocacy, decision-making domains, and successful shared governance initiatives (Hart, 1990; Karant, 1989; Lieberman, 1988) have also shed some light on leadership for shared governance. More specifically, a list of 23 leadership behaviors associated with teacher empowerment was reported in a recent study by Melenyzer (1990). Behaviors such as articulating a vision, providing teacher recognition, being visible, being decisive, supporting shared decision making, and demonstrating trust were identified with empowering leadership.

Empowerment also includes expanding teachers' knowledge base and enabling them to be free to reflect, thus enhancing their confidence about influencing how schools and classrooms will operate (Osterman & Kottkamp, 1993). (A discussion of supportive resources, including staff development programs, for teachers appears in Chapter 4.)

The Four Basic Questions

Viewing teachers as decision makers instead of "paper pushers" who perform bureaucratically designated steps in educating children, successful shared governance principals in our study allowed teachers to deal flexibly with uncertainty and complexity and supported them in taking risks without the threat of the consequences of failure. Conley (1988) argued that practitioners need to address four strategic questions *critical to the initial stages of structuring new forms of teacher participation* such as shared governance or site-based management:

> In which decisions will professional teachers become involved?
> Who will make what decisions in school site management?
> What are the basic tasks of administrators and teachers within the context of shared decision making?
> What is the role of teacher representatives, that is, unions, in school site decision making?

Addressing these and other such questions during the initiation and implementation of shared governance structures is helpful. However, an understanding of the strategies used by successful principals and the impacts of these strategies may be even more important to efforts to implement teacher empowerment. This book explores principals' strategies and their influence on the empowerment of teachers in shared governance schools. It also offers suggestions and caveats for implementing a shared governance approach in schools.

True Empowerment

As noted, the current research literature confirms that true empowerment extends well beyond participation in decision making; it also involves the elevation of *teachers as knowledgeable professionals.* Research indicates that empowerment requires the principal's trust and respect for teachers, support for staff development, support of teachers' decisions, and the adequate allocation of time for the development of collaborative relationships among teachers (Clift, Johnson, Holland, & Veal, 1992; Kasten, Short, & Jarmin, 1989). Empowerment further requires involvement by teachers *outside their own classrooms.* In effect, "true" empowerment includes decision participation, authority over issues concerning professional life both at the classroom level and at the school level, and opportunities to acquire knowledge necessary to warrant such authority (Kirby, 1991).

Shared governance (or site-based management) and empowerment of teachers—an integral component of school restructuring—presume autonomy of policymaking and administration vis-à-vis the district's central offices. It also requires participatory policymaking and administration at the individual school, and it demands what Goldman, Dunlap, and Conley (1993) call *facilitative power*: the ability to help others achieve a set of ends that may be shared, negotiated, or complementary.

Using facilitative power, educational leaders create favorable conditions for teachers to enhance their personal and collective performance. Such power is also manifested *through* someone, "resembling the images of electrical or ecological circuits of power . . . rather than images that describe objects (or people) being moved by force" (Goldman et al., 1993, p. 70). These authors argue that several *principal behaviors are essential to experimentation and to fundamental change in schools.* They suggest that principals (a) manifest a clear sense of purpose linked to a vision for the school, (b) use data to inform their decisions and the decisions of others, (c) allocate resources consistent with the school's vision, (d) help create new decision-making structures where they are needed, and (e) become more involved in indirect supporting roles for teachers and less involved in direct leadership activities (p. 89).

What results are likely to derive from teacher collaboration and true empowerment? Although research is sparse, empowerment has been associated with positive teacher morale and job satisfaction (Bacharach, Bamberger, Conley, & Bauer, 1990; David, 1989; Hawley, 1988), with commitment to school goals (Bacharach et al., 1990), and with student achievement (Hawley, 1988). In addition, Blase and Kirby's (1992) study of very effective principals who worked in "traditional" schools but who involved teachers in limited forms of shared decision making found that this process significantly strengthened support for decisions and improved faculty morale. Moreover, it resulted in *better* decisions because teachers shared formal and informal knowledge, creative ideas, and their experience.

Indeed, empowering teachers by implementing shared governance is more than the "in" thing for educators; rather, it may be *the best way to fulfill the school's mission and achieve its goals.* Furthermore, teachers in our study overwhelmingly indicated that (compared with all other sources of empowerment) principal leadership is the most important factor that contributes to teachers' empowerment.

Barriers to Teacher Empowerment

According to Kirby (1991), three key elements in the teacher empowerment formula are the ability to act (knowledge), the opportunity to act (decision participation), and the desire to act. However, on occasion, teachers who are given opportunities to involve themselves in schoolwide decisions often invest time and energy in trivial decisions and minor issues.

Weiss (1990) speculated that this occurs because teachers do not want to be involved in administrative decisions that they see as detractors from their classroom work and because they see empowerment as a sham. In other words, they believe participation in decision making is often made available as a way for them to vent their frustrations although they have little or no real impact on decision outcomes. In Weiss's view, under such conditions leadership fails to involve teachers in issues of importance, to give teachers authority, and to give teachers opportunities to expand their knowledge base.

What other barriers preclude changing traditional forms of decision making? Mutchler and Duttweiler (1990) cited organizational limitations, such as lack of definition and clarity regarding change efforts; inadequate or inappropriate resources; lack of hierarchical support; sources of resistance from school personnel, including the principal's or central office staff members' fear of losing power; and forms of teacher resistance, such as reluctance to change roles and responsibilities, lack of skills, and lack of trust.

The two latter limitations, administrators' fear of losing power and teacher resistance, appear to be especially potent and inhibiting factors. Similarly, mistakes in implementation of site-based management in Colorado schools included failure to define concepts, define roles, provide training and support, and understand organizational change processes (Harrison, Killion, & Mitchell, 1989).

About the Study

Can barriers to true teacher empowerment be overcome? What can we learn from the experiences of schools that have succeeded in their empowerment efforts? Little is known about the strategies used by principals *in shared governance schools*, strategies that directly and indirectly influence teacher empowerment. We sought to discover what successful shared governance principals do to develop an atmosphere of collegial, participative decision making. Such an atmosphere facilitates the complex act of teaching, unleashes teacher potential, supports innovation and risk taking, and increases students' intellectual and social development.

This book is based on data drawn from a qualitative study that investigated the broad question, *How do teachers perceive the characteristics of school principals that influence their sense of empowerment?* Data were collected and analyzed to generate descriptive categories, themes, and conceptual ideas. Consistent with open-ended research methods, no definitions of "successful leadership" or "empowerment" were presented on the questionnaire that teachers completed for the study. This would have limited the teachers' freedom to discuss their personal views of empowering principal behavior (Glaser, 1978; Glaser & Strauss, 1967). Our study also explored teachers' views about *why* they considered their principals' characteristics to be empowering and the *impacts* of school principals' behaviors on the cognitive, affective, and behavioral aspects of teachers' empowerment.

The open-ended questionnaire used to collect data was administered to 285 teachers in a select group of 11 schools—5 elementary, 3 middle, and 3 high schools—all of which have been members of the League of Professional Schools since its inception. As charter members of the League, these 11 schools began implementing shared governance structures and action research protocols in fall 1990. The League's purpose is to establish representative, democratic decision-making structures to promote teacher collaboration and involvement in schoolwide instructional and curricular decisions; the goal is improved teaching and learning. Governance structures deal with topics such as staff development, program innovation, classroom management, budgeting, and hiring. The League, however, does not specifically prescribe how member schools are to realize their commitment to shared governance; consequently, each school creates policies and procedures adapted to its unique situation.

Analysis of the teachers' data produced detailed descriptions of the empowering strategies used by shared governance principals, and this formed the database from which this book was written. *Successful principals* were those whose staffs had attained high levels of empowerment and participative decision making (shared governance) as defined by League criteria (e.g., educational focus, governance processes, and use of action research) and reflected in (a) annual reports, (b) on-site visitations, (c) teacher reports, and (d) facilitator (League staff member) reports. We chose to study only those principals who were considered *highly* successful (see Resource A for a full description of the research problem, sample, and procedures).

This book discusses the facilitative strategies used by successful principals in shared governance schools. The book describes some of the challenges of initiating shared governance as well as keys to success in shared governance. Suggestions for specific leadership behaviors are given, and the effects of shared decision making on the emotional, cognitive, and behavioral aspects of teachers' sense of empowerment are described. The book also examines the potential for developing a collaborative, reflective, problem-solving environment in schools in which "collegiality is an important strategy for bringing about the kinds of connections that make schools work and work well" (Sergiovanni, 1991, p. 138).

Chapters 2 and 3 describe two of the most fundamental strategies used by principals to promote teacher empowerment: building trust and creating enabling structures. Chapters 4 through 9 describe additional strategies and related practices that constitute the major dimensions of empowering leadership: support; encouragement of autonomy and innovation; personal dimensions; permitting risk and minimizing threat; rewards; and problem solving. The impact of each strategy on various dimensions of teachers' sense of empowerment is also discussed. Helpful hints and guidelines drawn from the study data are presented in the closing pages of each chapter.

We wish to emphasize that each of the successful empowering principals described by teachers used all of the strategies discussed in this book. Moreover, teachers in each school reported that principal leadership, as defined in terms of such strategies, was by far the largest contributor to teachers' sense of empowerment. All of the effects of these strategies on teachers (e.g., increase in self-esteem, satisfaction, and motivation) are considered aspects of empowerment.

Chapter 10, the final chapter, presents conclusions from our research and issues a challenge to practitioners to consider the use of empowering strategies in redesigning their schools. Recommendations for additional readings related to understanding new forms of leadership, teachers and their work, empowerment, and the initiation and implementation of shared governance structures are given in Resource B.

References

Apple, M. W. (1982). *Education and power.* Boston: Routledge & Kegan Paul.

Bacharach, S. B., Bamberger, P., Conley, S. C., & Bauer, S. (1990). The dimensionality of decision participation in educational organizations: The value of a multi-domain evaluation approach. *Educational Administration Quarterly, 26,* 126-167.

Barth, R. S. (1988). School: A community of leaders. In A. Lieberman (Ed.), *Building a professional culture in schools* (pp. 129-147). New York: Teachers College Press.

Blase, J., & Kirby, P. C. (1992). *Bringing out the best in teachers: What effective principals do.* Newbury Park, CA: Corwin.

Bolin, F. (1989). Empowering leadership. *Teachers College Record, 91*(1), 81-96.

Boyer, E. L. (1983). *High school: A report on secondary education in America.* New York: Harper & Row.

Bredeson, P. V. (1989). Redefining leadership and the roles of school principals: Responses to changes in the professional worklife of teachers. *The High School Journal, 73*(1), 9-20.

Carman, D. (1987). *A case study of a nationally recognized middle school's decentralized participatory governance structure.* Unpublished doctoral dissertation, Portland State University, Portland, OR.

Carnegie Forum on Education and the Economy, Task Force on Teaching as a Profession. (1986). *A nation prepared: Teachers for the 21st century*. New York: Carnegie Corporation.

Cherryholmes, C. (1988). *Power and criticism: Poststructural investigations in education*. New York: Teachers College Press.

Clift, R., Johnson, M., Holland, P., & Veal, M. L. (1992). Developing the potential for collaborative school leadership. *American Educational Research Journal, 29*(4), 877-908.

Conley, S. (1991). Review of research on teacher participation in school decision making. In G. Grant (Ed.), *Review of research in education* (pp. 225-266). Washington, DC: American Educational Research Association.

Conley, S. C. (1988, April). *From school site management to "participatory school site management."* Paper presented at the annual meeting of the American Educational Research Association, New Orleans.

David, J. L. (1989). Synthesis of research on school-based management. *Educational Leadership, 46*(8), 45-53.

Dunlap, D. M., & Goldman, P. (1991). Rethinking power in schools. *Educational Administration Quarterly, 27*(1), 5-29.

Education Commission of the States. (1986). *What's next? More leverage for teachers* (J. Green, Ed.). Denver, CO: Author.

Freire, P. (1985). *The politics of education*. South Hadley, MA: Bergin & Garvey.

Giroux, H. A., & McLaren, P. (1986). Teacher education and the politics of engagement: The case for democratic schooling. *Harvard Educational Review, 56*(3), 213-238.

Gladder, B. A. (1990). *Collaborative relationships in high schools: Implications for school reform*. Unpublished doctoral dissertation, University of Oregon, Eugene.

Glaser, B. G. (1978). *Theoretical sensitivity: Advances in the methodology of grounded theory*. Mill Valley, CA: Sociology Press.

Glaser, B. G., & Strauss, A. L. (1967). *The discovery of grounded theory: Strategies for qualitative research*. Chicago: Aldine.

Glickman, C. D. (1989). Has Sam and Samantha's time come at last? *Educational Leadership, 46*(9), 4-9.

Glickman, C. D. (1993). *Renewing America's schools: A guide for school-based action*. San Francisco: Jossey-Bass.

Goldman, P., Dunlap, D. M., & Conley, D. T. (1993). Facilitative power and nonstandardized solutions to school site restructuring. *Educational Administration Quarterly, 29*(1), 69-92.

Goodlad, J. I. (1984). *A place called school: Prospects for the future.* New York: McGraw-Hill.

Harrison, C. R., Killion, J. P., & Mitchell, J. E. (1989). Site based management: The realities of implementation. *Educational Leadership, 46*(8), 55-58.

Hart, A. W. (1990). Impacts of the school social unit on teacher authority during work redesign. *American Educational Research Journal, 27*(3), 503-532.

Hawley, W. D. (1988). Missing pieces of the educational reform agenda: Or, why the first and second waves may miss the boat. *Educational Administration Quarterly, 24*, 416-437.

Holmes Group Executive Board. (1986). *Tomorrow's teachers: A report of the Holmes Group.* East Lansing, MI: Author.

Immegart, G. L. (1988). Leadership and leader behavior. In N. J. Boyan (Ed.), *Handbook of research on educational administration* (pp. 259-277). New York: Longman.

Karant, V. I. (1989). Supervision in the age of teacher empowerment. *Educational Leadership, 46*(8), 27-29.

Kasten, K. L., Short, P. M., & Jarmin, H. (1989). Self-managing groups and the professional lives of teachers. *Urban Review, 21*(2), 63-80.

Kirby, P. C. (1991, April). *Shared decision making: Moving from concerns about rest rooms to concerns about classrooms.* Paper presented at the annual meeting of the American Educational Research Association, Chicago.

Kreisberg, S. (1992). *Transforming power: Domination, empowerment and education.* Albany: State University of New York Press.

Lieberman, A. (1988). Teachers and principals: Turf, tension and new tasks. *Phi Delta Kappan, 69*(9), 648-653.

Lightfoot, S. L. (1986). On goodness in schools: Themes of empowerment. *Peabody Journal of Education, 63*(3), 9-28.

Little, J. W. (1986). Seductive images and organizational realities in professional development. In A. Lieberman (Ed.), *Rethinking school improvement: Research, craft, and concept* (pp. 26-44). New York: Teachers College Press.

Maeroff, G. I. (1988). Blueprint for empowering teachers. *Phi Delta Kappan, 69*(7), 473-477.

Malen, B., & Ogawa, R. (1988). Professional-patron influence on site-based governance councils: A confounding case study. *Educational Evaluation and Policy Analysis, 10*(4), 251-270.

McLaren, P. (1988). Language, social structure and the production of subjectivity. *Critical Pedagogy Networker, 1*(2-3), 1-10.

Melenyzer, B. J. (1990, November). *Teacher empowerment: The discourse, meanings, and social actions of teachers.* Paper presented at the annual conference of the National Council of States on Inservice Education, Orlando, FL.

Mutchler, S. E., & Duttweiler, P. C. (1990, April). *Implementing shared decision making in school based management: Barriers to changing traditional behavior.* Paper presented at the annual meeting of the American Educational Research Association, Boston.

National Commission on Excellence in Education. (1983). *A nation at risk: The imperative for educational reform.* Washington, DC: U.S. Government Printing Office.

Osterman, K. F. (1989, April). *Supervision and shared authority: A study of principal and teacher control in six urban middle schools.* Paper presented at the annual meeting of the American Educational Research Association, San Francisco.

Osterman, K. F., & Kottkamp, R. B. (1993). *Reflective practice for educators.* Newbury Park, CA: Corwin.

Reitzug, U. C. (1994). A case study of empowering principal behavior. *American Educational Research Journal, 31*(2), 283-307.

Sergiovanni, T. J. (1989). *Schooling for tomorrow: Directing reforms to issues that count.* Needham Heights, MA: Allyn & Bacon.

Sergiovanni, T. J. (1991). *The principalship: A reflective practice perspective* (2nd ed.). Boston: Allyn & Bacon.

Simpson, G. W. (1989). *Change masters in schools: A description of innovative strategies in Texas and Michigan.* Unpublished doctoral dissertation, Texas A & M University, College Station.

Sizer, T. K. (1984). *Horace's compromise: The dilemma of the American high school.* Boston: Houghton Mifflin.

Spring, J. (1988). *Conflict of interest: Politics and power in education.* New York: Longman.

Tate, P. M. (1991, April). *A resource allocation perspective on teacher empowerment.* Paper presented at the annual meeting of the American Educational Research Association, Chicago.

Weiss, C. (1990, April). *How much shared leadership is there in public high schools?* Paper presented at the annual meeting of the American Educational Research Association, Boston.

Wise, A. (1986). Graduate teacher education and teacher professionalism. *Journal of Teacher Education, 37*(5), 36-40.

2

Trusting the Experts

TEACHERS

I think that the principal's willingness to give up some power shows a great deal of respect for the teachers. She brought the idea of shared governance to our school and she fully supports our shared governance group.

—Middle School Teacher

Empowerment is a characteristic of very secure administrators who are comfortable trusting others. Empowering your personnel gives them feelings of worth and value, of importance.

—Middle School Teacher

Our study data suggest that trust is the foundation for shared governance and teacher empowerment. Trust has been defined as a quality that "is built very slowly and in small increments, is established more by deeds than by words, and is sustained by openness in interpersonal relations" (Schmuck & Runkel, 1985, p. 98). McGregor (1967) defines trust as the knowledge that one person will not take unfair advantage of another person, deliberately or consciously; further, any harm committed accidentally or unconsciously is always expected to be repaired.

People who believe that others are motivated to protect and nurture their relationships are apt to be trusting. Yet in daily encounters with our colleagues we often respond to one another in "binding" not "freeing" ways. That is, instead of listening carefully, validating our impressions, and honestly reporting our feelings and opinions, we interpret each other's behavior, demand things of each other, claim to know each other's motivations, and force obligations on each other. This is unfortunate because the degree of trust among people affects the types of problems people are willing to share. Without trust, people are likely to say only those things they expect others want to hear (Lovell & Wiles, 1983).

In this chapter we discuss this elusive yet essential aspect of a group's cohesion and demonstrate how it fosters cooperation and effective communication, two essential aspects of empowerment. We first describe some fundamental aspects of trust and describe how shared governance principals build trust, according to reports from teachers who participated in our study.

Imagine you are part of a small group of teachers about to discuss department budget allocations for the coming school year. You may be thinking, "If I am open, honestly sharing my opinions and feelings, will I be accepted and supported? Will others reciprocate with honest communications? Or will what I say be used against me if the others do not agree with me?" You would know intuitively that sharing your thoughts, ideas, and personal resources can involve considerable risk.

Johnson and Johnson (1987) note, "When the trust level is low, group members will be evasive, dishonest, and inconsiderate in their communications" (p. 420). These authors describe cooperative group work, essential to the effective operation of a school, as encompassing both *trusting behavior* (openness and sharing) and *trustworthy behavior* (the expression of acceptance, support, and cooperative intentions). Our data show that in effective shared governance schools, members recognize their interdependence and strive to protect their trusting relationships. They also realize that trust is a "fragile quality on which a single action can have profoundly destructive consequences" (Schmuck & Runkel, 1985, p. 98).

Why Do We Need Trust

To be fully effective professionals, we must feel that we work in an environment of trust. As Covey (1989) explains in his recent best-selling book, *The Seven Habits of Highly Effective People,* trust is the amount of "safeness" we feel with others. If we feel safe with others, we are able to sit with them and comfortably discuss difficult or delicate issues about our work and our performance. We are able to reveal ourselves as we strive to manage both personal and professional challenges. In an atmosphere of trust *we are able to work together to identify and solve our problems.* This is the kind of environment that shared governance principals foster in schools; yet for most members of school communities it is still an ideal instead of a reality.

Without trust, people are likely to close up, to keep to themselves, to even close ranks in cliques or special interest groups. Without trust, issues are seldom discussed and never resolved. Without trust, a school cannot improve and grow into the rich, nurturing microsociety needed by children and adults alike. The reward of a trusting environment is immeasurable, yet the price of a lack of trust is dear.

The Essentials

Building trust takes effort and sincerity. For many people, trust may come easily, merely from being given the opportunity to work closely with others on real problems. For others, trust comes more slowly due to personal experiences or other matters beyond one's immediate control. As successful shared governance principals demonstrate, the challenge is to *build* a trusting environment by (a) encouraging openness, (b) facilitating effective communication, and (c) modeling understanding, the cornerstone of trust.

Encouraging Openness

To understand how interpersonal openness can be encouraged, consider a model called the Johari window, which was derived from theories of personality and social psychology. The Johari window has four quadrants that represent varying levels of individual behavior, feelings, and motivation that may be known (or unknown) to one's self and known (or unknown) to others. Each person has areas that are *open* to the world (known by self and others), *blind* areas (unknown by self but known by others), *hidden* areas (known by self but not by others), and *unknown* areas (unknown by self and others) (Luft, 1961). People who develop and realize their potential have great self-awareness and openness; they strive to increase openness and limit hidden, unknown, or blind areas of their personalities.

In our study, we found that shared governance principals are open, ever growing, problem-solving people who derive satisfaction from being with others. They de-emphasize status differences, believe in equality among professionals, and know that *people flourish when they feel free.* They encourage or build trust by personally modeling openness in all interactions with faculty and staff members. In addition, shared governance teams, knowing that the quality of human understanding is the core of human interaction, consistently call attention to the ongoing processes of their groups and strive to achieve accurate perceptions, mutual understanding, and acceptance of others. *Acceptance,* in particular, is fundamental to interpersonal openness:

> To welcome or at least accept from other individuals every kind and form of behavior called forth by the tensions which occur in problem situations is to have a basis for better understanding and communication. If varied behaviors are not accepted, or, in other words, if they are screened out or rejected by either direct or subtle means, the other person's defenses may be mobilized, resentments precipitated, and the channel of communications closed. (Lucio & McNeil, 1969, p. 97)

Clearly, the power of honest, open, and accepting communication cannot be overemphasized in developing trust.

Facilitating Effective Communication

Schmuck and Runkel (1985) describe six skills identified with successful interpersonal communication: *paraphrasing* (checking your understanding of the other person's meaning), *impression checking*

(checking your impression of the other person's feelings), *describing the other's behavior, describing your own behavior, making clear statements of your own ideas,* and *describing your own feelings* (p. 99). The key to becoming adept at communication is to practice these skills. Every new situation and relationship requires that one call on these skills; group work is the most challenging situation.

Two of these six skills, paraphrasing and impression checking, as well as the key skills of active listening and giving I-messages, are described by Roberts (1991) in a staff development guide published by the National Association of Secondary School Principals:

- *Active listening* is attending to the person who is speaking to you, and hearing what is intended.
- *Paraphrasing* is checking your understanding of a speaker's *meaning.*
- *Impression checking* is confirming or correcting your understanding of a speaker's *feelings.*
- *Giving an I-message* is letting someone know your response to his or her behaviors as clearly and unambiguously as possible. It includes a statement describing the other's behavior, your resulting feeling, and the effect on you (positive or negative).

Roberts notes that lack of ability in any or all of the key areas can inhibit or confound problem solving, reduce trust, and magnify feelings of isolation among administrators, teachers, and support personnel.

Again, our data demonstrate that successful shared governance principals are skilled in facilitating effective communication through the use of such skills; they also act as *models* of effective communication for others.

Modeling Understanding

As noted, the virtual cornerstone of trust is understanding. Covey (1989) asserts that we have achieved deep understanding if we can look at issues from another person's point of view and even argue his or her case! Of course, we are not going to agree on all things, as our lives are complex and our differences great, including our values, goals, and expectations, but we do have the power to listen carefully, ask clarifying questions, and ask to be heard in return. This type of interaction paves the way for better understanding of one another.

As you might expect, shared governance leaders *model* this kind of understanding and, by virtue of this consistent demonstration of understanding, help others to come to the same behaviors. For example, we noted that shared governance principals gently but assertively ensure that all parties are heard on issues being discussed. These leaders did not tolerate interruptions while someone was speaking, and they modeled deep understanding of each person's contributions by listening attentively and responding appropriately.

Three Important Caveats

As shared governance principals strive to build trust by encouraging openness, facilitating effective communication, and modeling understanding, they keep three factors in mind: Skills must be *practiced, conflict* is likely to occur, and teacher-leaders must also be *learners.*

The Importance of Practice

As noted earlier, Kirby (1991) has demonstrated that true teacher empowerment involves (a) decision participation, (b) authority over issues concerning professional life both at the classroom and at school levels, and (c) opportunities to acquire knowledge necessary to warrant such authority. She further notes that "an empowered faculty may create structures to allow collaborative planning and decision making, but it also receives the necessary training and support to develop as a group and to acquire expertise on policy issues under consideration" (pp. 3-4). Thus two commitments must be made if a group is to work well: Group members must learn their roles and responsibilities, and *they must practice their process skills.* In a related article in which she discusses the barriers to empowering leadership, Bolin (1989) warns that

the administrator should never make the mistake of putting
teachers together in groups to work out solutions to a problem without taking time to develop appropriate group
process skills. A faculty, left alone, will not automatically function in a democratic, cooperative manner. In fact, left alone,
it is more likely to become chaotic or divide into factions led
by various autocratic members. (p. 90)

The shared governance principals described in our study consistently provided training in group process skills. They also regularly
involved teachers in democratic, collaborative activities that increased teachers' ability and desire to cooperate in the future. In
addition, these leaders realized that making the connection between
the practiced skills and the everyday interpersonal functioning of
faculty and staff members was essential. They also understood that
consistent use of the skills yielded improvements in problem-
solving efforts, group work, and interpersonal trust.

The results of such efforts were typically impressive. Indeed, it
was this kind of collaboration, this engagement in social responsibility and commitment, that helped teachers realize great possibilities for their schools. Such involvement also allowed teachers to be
creative, to avoid standard solutions or bureaucratic approaches to
complex problems, and to achieve personal and social freedom.
Maxine Greene (1988), the respected educator-philosopher, has said,
"Freedom shows itself or comes into being when individuals come
together in a particular way, when they are authentically present to
one another (without masks, pretenses, badges of office), when they
have a project they can mutually pursue" (p. 16). We must remember
that it is preparation and gradual, authentic involvement that makes
teacher reflection and responsible action possible.

The Likelihood of Conflict

Conflict is inevitable. In fact, many types of conflict are considered normal, and even necessary, for organizational change and
improvement! In an open atmosphere characterized by interpersonal respect and understanding, our differences naturally emerge
and are "put on the table." This allows us to discuss our problems

and to explore alternative ways to resolve them. With good communication, we are able to work through our conflicts and create better schools where all concerns, ideas, and needs are respected and where all people strive to be their best.

Indeed, conflict is not necessarily a negative force; it can be an opportunity for both growth and mutual support among professionals who most often work in isolation. Little (1993), one of the first scholars to examine teacher collegiality, proposed that professional development among teachers become *an opportunity for informed dissent*:

> Admittedly, deeply felt differences in value and belief can make agreements both difficult to achieve and unstable over time. At its extreme, dissent may engender a certain micropolitical paralysis, while shared commitments may enable people to take bold action. Nonetheless, to permit or even foster principled dissent (e.g., by structuring devil's advocate roles and arguments) places a premium on the evaluation of alternatives and the close scrutiny of underlying assumptions. (p. 138)

In the positive sense, then, conflict can frequently lead to a win-win outcome rather than a situation in which someone ends up ahead and someone ends up behind. In their popular book, *Getting to Yes*, Fisher and Ury (1981) offer a concise, proven strategy for coming to mutually acceptable agreements in all types of conflict. They suggest these methods for handling disagreements:

- Separate people from problems
- Focus on people's interests rather than on positions that are rigidly held
- Establish precise goals at the onset of discussions
- Work together to invent creative options that will satisfy the interests of all parties

From our study, it is clear that successful shared governance principals understand and even *welcome* conflict as a way to produce substantive, positive outcomes over the long run. Regarding conflict

as potentially *constructive* helps build supportive human relationships because it allows us to deal with our differences in win-win ways.

The Leader as Learner

In *Building a Professional Culture in Schools*, Lieberman, Saxl, and
Miles (1988) discuss the dilemma of teacher-leaders who work in
restructured schools. Interestingly, the combination of being a colleague and also being an appointed leader or "expert" is just as
challenging in terms of building trust among fellow educators as it
is in more traditional arrangements. The authors suggest that teacher-
leaders must learn that the tensions of negotiating from a position
of leadership without threatening those in existing administrative
positions (especially in a school with little precedent for teacher
leadership) are an inevitable result of the movement to profession-
alize schools and of the overall process of change itself. In addition,
it is also possible for *other teachers* to feel threatened by teacher-leaders,
who are perceived as both "trying to get ahead" and maintaining
deep commitments to education.

Lieberman et al. (1988) suggest that teacher-leaders engage in
supportive communication (thereby building trust), build a support
group, develop shared influence, and, in effect, build a set of productive relationships. No matter what the size of the school, the age
or experience of the staff, or the program design, these same skills
can be used to legitimate the leadership role, just as they are typically
used by effective shared governance principals. Thus as schools
evolve throughout reform efforts we may find that *all* educators
need to develop a process of building trust among their colleagues.

How Shared Governance
Principals Build Trust and Empower Teachers

The shared governance principals in our study were relentless in
their efforts to build and support an environment of trust in their
schools. Besides their consistent efforts to develop openness, viable
communication, and mutual support (often through carefully planned

staff development sessions) these principals used other powerful methods to *demonstrate* their trust in teachers' professional judgment.

Encouraging Teacher Involvement

Successful shared governance principals show trust in teachers' capacity for responsible involvement in both school-level and classroom-level decision making. Words such as "trust," "respect," and "confidence" were used to describe principals who not only *permitted* but *encouraged* and even *expected* teachers to make decisions and implement actions related to instructional and, to a lesser degree, noninstructional areas of work. Furthermore, these principals protected *dissent* among teachers during discussions of school issues. One teacher commented,

> The principal conveys a deep sense of trust in my personal and professional judgment. *I might suggest an unusual approach* to a skill or concept and the response will likely be, "Do it." These responses are genuine, not off-handed, and through them I sense a willingness on her part to assign decision-making to me. (emphasis added)

In effect, principals strongly encouraged teachers to participate in formal shared governance structures and informal processes available for schoolwide decision making. Not surprising, our data indicate, however, that decisions or actions associated with individual teachers' *classrooms* were emphasized somewhat. One teacher noted, "[She] trusted me to instruct and work with our students in a manner that was compatible to the needs of my students." Another said, "I was trusted to make decisions about methods of instruction that would benefit my students."

Eliminating Intimidation

Our data indicate that principals enhanced trust in teachers by working to create school climates free of intimidation, fear, coercion, and criticism. Principals also generally refrained from actions that teachers believed contradicted the basic principles of shared governance:

> She does not breathe down my neck constantly; she gives me the freedom to pursue goals in a nonthreatening atmosphere.

> She values my opinions and ideas and allows me to share them with her without fear of reprisal or criticism even when our opinions differ.

Successful shared governance principals sense that the school's success lies in the skills and attitudes of the professional staff, not merely within the leadership capabilities of the principal: "[She] promoted the notion that teachers were knowledgeable about their field and that they could be trusted to do what is best for children." Such principals feel that teachers *can* and *should* be trusted to do what is best for students. (Related issues of *risk* and *threat* are discussed in Chapter 7.)

Subtly Facilitating Empowerment

Although shared governance principals conveyed substantial trust in teachers, our findings also reveal that they "actively" influenced teachers through a variety of indirect and direct, yet unobtrusive, means. Such attempts were often directed at facilitating teacher empowerment, of course, rather than controlling teachers to comply with principal-determined goals.

For example, principals articulated expectations and communicated their opinions and thoughts as *equal*, not superior, members in school governance discussions. One teacher noted this when he said, "She accepts the teachers as fellow professionals." These principals indirectly also "guided," "encouraged," "questioned," "praised," and "supported" teachers so as to enhance their empowerment in shared governance schools. Clearly, communicating trust to teachers as true professionals was, according to our data, a fundamental element in the empowering and trust-building process:

As a teacher who has worked with children for 16+ years, I feel that I do have a great deal of hands-on experience that is invaluable when assisting future curriculum changes. Not to be involved in decisions (grouping, curriculum, etc.) would be an insult and would have made me feel very useless and frustrated.

Benefits of Building Trust

Building trust is critical to empowering teachers. In their recent study of effective traditional principals, Blase and Kirby (1992) found that extending autonomy to teachers had quite positive effects on their attitudes and performance. Whether principals' attempts to support teacher autonomy and to avoid intruding into the instructional realm of teachers are due primarily to structural and psychological barriers (Meyer & Rowan, 1977) or to principals' belief in the true professionalism of teachers is not yet clear. In any event, teachers consistently associate autonomy with professionalism and trust in their judgment.

We found that the successful shared governance principals in our study demonstrated their trust in teachers' professional abilities in many of the same ways described by Blase and Kirby (1992). They granted professional autonomy, particularly in instructional matters, and they used more proactive strategies such as conveying expectations, involving groups in schoolwide decisions, and providing opportunities for professional development. Moreover, they demonstrated individual integrity (honesty and openness) in all personal encounters.

All of these approaches have the effect of making teachers feel "satisfied," "motivated," and "confident." Because of the atmosphere of trust, teachers are more likely to work harder, be optimistic, and feel a sense of professionalism. Principal-teacher and teacher-teacher relationships seem to improve as well. From our data we learned that an environment of trust raises teachers' self-esteem, commitment, and sense of ownership. All of the impacts described above constitute dimensions of teacher empowerment that are directly enhanced by shared governance principals.

Reminders

Successful shared governance principals demonstrate a remarkable ability to build and maintain trust among professional staff members. In many cases, the strategies they use to establish trust are developed *over time* in a learning process that may include mistakes as well as successes. Clearly, no simple checklist can guide principals in this endeavor, but the following reminders may be helpful to leaders involved in the empowerment of teachers:

1. Listen with respect.

When you listen, do so sincerely. Do more than merely hear others; strive to truly understand their points of view. Ask yourself, "Could I fairly represent this person's perspective?" Remember that what is important to others should also be important to you and expect that all members of the school community recognize and demonstrate this.

2. Be a model of trust.

Demonstrate daily your trust in teachers' professional judgment. (They are, after all, closer to the work of educating children; as such, they are the experts!) Model confidence in others and extend to them respect, courtesy, and consideration; furthermore, accept no less from the professional staff. This is the *essence* of building trust.

3. Help others to communicate effectively.

If necessary, sponsor staff development sessions so that faculty and staff members can *learn about and practice the skills of effective communication and conflict resolution.*

4. Clarify expectations.

Everyone needs to understand clearly who is responsible for what. Knowing one's own responsibilities and the responsibilities of others frees people to attack problems creatively and work toward the goal of school improvement.

5. Celebrate experimentation and support risk.

Growth and improvement necessarily come from trying new ways to do things. When teachers know that efforts with an element of risk will be supported (and that not-so-successful efforts will be accepted as part of the improvement process), they are more likely to tap into creative, new ways to do important things. In addition, shared governance principals "keep teachers safe" during experimentation by occasionally absorbing the penalties or "fallout" that emerges from risks taken (see Chapter 5 for a discussion of *autonomy* and *innovation* and Chapter 7 for a discussion of *risk* and *threat*).

6. Exhibit personal integrity.

Honesty, straightforwardness, and the offering of sincere apologies when warranted do much to build trust among those with whom you work.

References

Blase, J., & Kirby, P. C. (1992). *Bringing out the best in teachers: What effective principals do.* Newbury Park, CA: Corwin.

Bolin, F. S. (1989). Empowering leadership. *Teachers College Record, 91*(1), 81-96.

Covey, S. R. (1989). *The seven habits of highly effective people: Restoring the character ethic.* New York: Simon & Schuster.

Fisher, R., & Ury, W. (1981). *Getting to yes: Negotiating agreement without giving in.* Boston: Houghton Mifflin.

Greene, M. (1988). *Dialectic of freedom.* New York: Teachers College Press.

Johnson, D. W., & Johnson, F. P. (1987). *Joining together: Group theory and group skills* (3rd ed.). Englewood Cliffs, NJ: Prentice Hall.

Kirby, P. C. (1991, April). *Shared decision making: Moving from concerns about restrooms to concerns about classrooms.* Paper presented at

the annual meeting of the American Educational Research Association, Chicago.

Lieberman, A., Saxl, E. R., & Miles, M. B. (1988). Teacher leadership:
Ideology and practice. In A. Lieberman (Ed.), *Building a professional
culture in schools* (pp. 148-166). New York: Teachers College Press.

Little, J. W. (1993). Teachers' professional development in a climate
of educational reform. *Educational Evaluation and Policy Analysis, 15*(2), 129-151.

Lovell, J. T., & Wiles, K. (1983). *Supervision for better schools* (5th ed.).
Englewood Cliffs, NJ: Prentice Hall.

Lucio, W. H., & McNeil, J. D. (1969). *Supervision: A synthesis of thought
and action.* New York: McGraw-Hill.

Luft, J. (1961). The Johari window: A graphic model of awareness in
interpersonal behavior. *Human Relations Training News, 5*(1), 6-7.

McGregor, D. (1967). *The professional manager.* New York: McGraw-
Hill.

Meyer, J. W., & Rowan, B. (1977). Institutionalized organizations:
Formal structure as myth and ceremony. *American Journal of Sociology, 83,* 440-463.

Roberts, J. (1991). *How to improve communication: A staff development
mini-session.* Reston, VA: National Association of Secondary
School Principals.

Schmuck, R. A., & Runkel, P. J. (1985). *The handbook of organizational
development in schools* (3rd ed.). Palo Alto, CA: Mayfield.

3

Creating Structures
That Help Teachers Do Their Best

> We have formed teams to research new ways to improve our
> students' education. Working in these teams, we do the research
> and we make the decisions. . . . I think the idea of faculty empow-
> erment is necessary to improve morale. I feel lucky to have a
> principal that gives the faculty freedom and power to control the
> destiny of education in our school.
>
> —High School Teacher

Becoming part of a project of teacher empowerment challenges educators to rethink their day-to-day practices, their values, and their
beliefs. In a collegial, collaborative environment, principals consistently concentrate on *enabling others* to examine and redesign schools
for improved learning, and teachers learn to share power and work
as a team. This is a significant change from the traditional, bureaucratic, controlling ways of operating in many schools, and it reflects
the belief, even the assumption, that teachers are capable of an exciting,
new, transformative vision of teaching.

Successful shared governance principals realize that increasing
teacher access to decision making is essential to empowering teachers and that cooperative decision making is the foundation of shared

governance (Maeroff, 1988a, 1988b). However, shared governance does not happen only because an open-minded principal decides to involve people in those decisions affecting them; it happens when a school is carefully and systematically *structured* to encourage authentic collaboration.

Research into teacher collaboration projects indicates that successful projects are linked to active administrative support, recognition of teachers, and availability of time for collaboration (Flinders, 1988). Most important, certain structures have been shown to enhance shared decision making (Little, 1987; McNeil, 1988). The teachers in our study underscore the importance of initiating leadership by teachers in ways that exceed mere delegation of administrative responsibility, identification of lead teachers, and other conservative measures (see, e.g., Barth, 1988; Bolin, 1989; Goodlad, 1984; Joyce, 1986; Sizer, 1984). In fact, our study argues the need for a complete rethinking of the role of the teacher, the role of the principal, and the day-to-day operations of the school.

Teachers know that greater overall participation leads to job satisfaction (Bird & Little, 1986) and that they are capable of making important decisions in complicated situations for the interests of students (Schön, 1987). In fact, our data suggest that teachers recognize the deep, moral dimensions and value-laden nature of teaching (Bolin, 1989; Greene, 1988), that they stand opposed to their current relative powerlessness and isolation, and that they are ready to reassert themselves to meet the challenge of shared governance. As one teacher said,

> Our principal involves every faculty member in educational decisions and believes that we are capable of making intelligent decisions. Shared decision making makes me feel empowered. I am more involved in school matters and feel the need to keep abreast of current educational issues. I communicate more with my colleagues and find myself eager to attend meetings because I know I will be actively participating rather than passively listening.

Readiness, Common Goals,
and Unique Characteristics

We found that successful shared governance principals demonstrate the initiative to liberate teachers from bureaucratic domination as well as an inclination to reconstruct teaching as a profession that reflects the democratic ideals of liberty and self-governance (for reflections on these ideas, see Strike, 1993). These principals at the same time provide the *platform* and *appropriate support* for shared governance structures to be successful. This means that they (a) determine the school's *readiness* (R), (b) work to establish common *goals* (G), and (c) respond to the school's *unique characteristics* (U) as they proceed. This "R-G-U" approach was apparent among the principals in our study.

Readiness

The degree of readiness established in schools is one of the best predictors of the level of teacher participation and level of teacher empowerment (Bredeson, 1989). Roberts (1991) recently studied the readiness of prospective members of the Georgia League of Professional Schools to engage in shared decision making. The schools specifically focused on core educational activities, such as teaching and learning, and illuminated their work by the use of action research (the collection, analysis, and interpretation of data to improve decision making). (Many of the principals of these same schools later joined the League; several of their schools participated in the study described in this book.)

Roberts used survey questions and document analysis to investigate the work of 214 teachers and administrators (representing 42 schools) attending League regional orientation and planning sessions. She determined *readiness levels* and predicted success of participating schools by the use of a conceptual framework derived from theories of change in organizations. This framework includes implementability of innovation, leadership strength, stages of concern/levels of use, and collegial interaction, as described below.

Implementability of Innovation

Roberts determined it was possible to implement an innovation when the following conditions prevailed:

- The school's *needs* matched the shared governance project goals (or at least an awareness of the need for increased teacher involvement).
- The definition, purposes, and procedures associated with the shared governance approach were *clear.*
- The *complexity*, or level of challenge, associated with attempting new ways of operating was related to project success. Greater learning and change resulted from attempting more difficult changes.
- The project's goals were viewed as *practical*. Practical concerns were addressed by several questions: Did the shared governance goals fit the organizational realities of the school? Would availability of time or existing school and district regulations conflict with the project goals? Were the project goals relevant to the participants' concerns?

Leadership Strength

Roberts found that leadership strength was specifically related to (a) obtaining resources, (b) buffering the shared governance efforts from outside interference, (c) encouraging the staff along the lines of school improvement and shared governance principles, and (d) adapting daily operating procedures to new initiatives. Active principal support is clearly related to the success of change efforts (Hall & Hord, 1984).

Stages of Concern and Levels of Use

Roberts (1991) concluded that the more advanced the stage of concern and the higher the level of actual use of shared governance approaches on the part of teachers the greater the chance of successful implementation of shared governance principles in a school (for details about these concepts, see Hall, Loucks, Rutherford, & Newlove, 1975; Hall, Wallace, & Dorsett, 1973).

Stages of Concern	*Levels of Use*
Being aware of the innovation	Nonuse
Desiring information about it	Becoming oriented to the innovation
Considering how to personalize its use	Preparation for its use
	Mechanical use
Deliberating on its management	Routine use
Considering its consequences	Refinement of its use
Engaging in collaborating about it	Integration of its use with other concepts and programs
Refocusing ways of implementing the innovation	Renewal or redesign of the innovation

Collegial Interaction

In successful shared governance projects, Roberts (1991) found, teachers frequently discussed and made decisions related to instruction in such schools and were frequently the source of incentives and, consequently, a major factor in determining a school's readiness for shared governance. Other studies have confirmed that teacher isolation, limited interaction, and infrequent discussions about instruction are detrimental to shared governance efforts.

Not surprising, Roberts found that the typical barriers to organizational change were evident in schools that were less successful in their shared governance efforts. Such barriers include the following:

- A lack of commitment to the change to shared governance
- Inadequate feedback on progress related to the change
- Resistance to change in general
- Inadequate knowledge or skills for implementing the change
- Vested interest in the status quo

- Threat or fear of new situations or ways of operating
- Lack of support or endorsement from significant persons
- Inadequate expertise for solving problems arising during initiation and implementation (see Lovell & Wiles, 1983)

Roberts (1991) concluded that three fourths of the schools that succeeded in implementing shared governance in accordance with the League's principles exhibited substantial *readiness* according to at least *four* of the above-mentioned factors (implementability, leadership strength, stage of concern attained/level of use attained, and collegial interaction). Such schools also exhibited *few barriers to change*. In the less successful schools, for example, specific barriers included the following:

- Top-down operations
- Feeling "rudderless" or lacking in group development
- Lack of time and/or money
- Lack of consensus, team effort, or administrator encouragement
- New leadership and/or instability
- Recent traumas
- Central office interference, dictating, or resistance to change
- Teacher resistance or entrenchment
- Poor timing for project consideration

Our findings in regard to readiness are remarkably consistent with those of Roberts. Shared governance principals behaved in ways that were largely congruent with the readiness factors delineated above. Clearly, school leaders embarking on shared governance efforts should make concerted attempts to *enhance readiness* (which includes *impeding barriers* to organizational change) along the lines described in the above framework.

Common Goals

The establishment of common goals, identified through reflective and collaborative discussions among teachers and staff members, is a second factor essential to successfully implementing shared governance structures. Such discussion must first focus on *instructional matters*, in contrast to less significant administrative and operational issues.

In his recent book, *Renewing America's Schools*, Glickman (1993) outlines a philosophical and policy model for shared governance. This model has two essential elements: (a) a consistent focus on what Glickman calls the "educational tasks" of curriculum: staff development, coaching, instructional programs, student assessment, and the instructional budget; and (b) a three-dimensional framework for supporting school renewal, which involves a *charter* (specifics of governance for making democratic, schoolwide educational decisions), a *critical-study process* (systematic collection and analysis of student data for setting learning priorities), and a *covenant* (addressing the principles of learning, which provides consistency of educational purpose).

This approach has proved successful in many shared governance schools. It ensures that all faculty and staff members agree on the goals (as well as procedures) for the school, and it buffers and protects the shared governance principles of operation during times of administrative/bureaucratic change. Thus the gains made under the new way of operating are safeguarded.

Your Unique School

Understanding the *unique* characteristics of the school is another factor essential to successful implementation of shared governance. Because every school is unique and because every school has different people and a different social, cultural, and political context, no single approach to shared governance can be considered the "right" approach. Do not simply adopt methods or procedures that have worked elsewhere; instead, adapt to your needs those ideas that seem to hold promise for your particular set of circumstances. As we will see, teachers in our study reported an array of approaches, policies, and procedures, all particularly suited to their needs.

Guideposts for Beginning Shared Governance

Without implying that you must begin shared governance efforts *in one particular way*, we describe here (a) four typical alternative models of schoolwide decision making and (b) a fifth approach, the "shared governance council," which we derived from our data and which we call an effective "collective" design for schoolwide decision making. The main features of a "collective" model of shared governance reflect what the successful principals in our study used. But first we review typical alternative models to shared governance. Remember, the following review of alternatives and general design is merely meant to provide you with *guideposts* along the way to initiating and implementing shared governance in your school.

Alternative Models

Drawing on a review of research and their own field experiences, Hallinger and Richardson (1988) produced a conceptual analysis of organizational models that involve teachers in schoolwide decision making. The four distinct models they present—the Principal's Advisory Council, the School Improvement Team, the Instructional Support Team, and the Lead Teacher Committee—vary in terms of purpose, teacher and principal roles, and impacts.

The **Principal's Advisory Council** is a group of elected faculty members that acts in an advisory capacity to the principal. This group tends to focus on the policy and management domain rather than on instructional matters; its mission is less oriented to instructional improvement than are other models.

The **School Improvement Team** is a school-site council of teachers and parents working with the principal for schoolwide improvement. Common goals are adopted, and the team has some budgetary authority. Although this model is most frequently associated with school-based management initiatives, drawbacks are the lack of (a) teacher-to-teacher interaction; (b) schoolwide instructional focus (as is found in the Instructional Support Team described below); and (c) ongoing, joint problem solving on instructional issues.

The **Instructional Support Team** is composed of volunteer or principal-appointed interdisciplinary staff members with a mission of dealing with schoolwide *instructional* matters. The focus includes learning problems, curriculum, and instructional improvement. The team meets on a regular basis, exists primarily to improve learning conditions for students, and relies heavily on the expertise of its members. Principals convey to faculty the importance of the team, work directly with the team, and rely on it for advice and assistance.

The **Lead Teacher Committee** is the most comprehensive school-based decision-making design. This committee is delegated formal authority by the Board of Education; members of the committee are involved in teacher orientation and administrative and instructional mentoring matters. Committee members have formal voice in policy-making, and they accept wide accountability for educational results with students. Most of the existing literature about this model consists of prescriptive proposals.

The preceding concepts describe alternatives for schoolwide decision making with diverse strengths and weaknesses. However, these concepts were derived from previous research and field-based experiences rather than from current empirical studies of schools specifically engaged in shared governance initiatives. The results of our study and projects conducted within the Georgia League of Professional Schools (Glickman & Allen, 1992-1993) reflect a *combination* of the design elements noted above and appear to produce excellent results for shared decision making in today's varied school settings. As mentioned earlier, successful shared governance principals implement hybrid designs adapted to their particular school situation. Generally, these designs include the features described below.

An Effective Design for a Shared Governance Council

In shared governance schools, the following elements characterize what is typically called the *Teachers' Council* or the *Shared Governance Council*. In actuality, each school involved in the League of Professional Schools assigns different labels to various elements of the shared governance design.

Impetus—A faculty/staff/parent/student council is formed under the leadership and support of the principal *or* by teachers with the principal's agreement. In rare cases, a district dictates a shared governance initiative.

Membership—Members of the council are elected or, less frequently, appointed by the principal in the early months. Infrequently, council members are the department or grade-level chairpersons, or the chairpersons may serve *in concert* with the regular council members.

Representation—Members of the council represent the school community at large, and each member's liaison group is formed randomly, with faculty, staff, parents, and students participating. *Committee* membership is voluntary, allowing people to choose to participate on committees of interest.

Scope of Authority—Effective shared governance principals extend advisory and/or decision-making rights to representatives and their groups, according to agreements. Clarification of areas of advice and decision making occurs early in a shared governance initiative; however, the formality of such agreements varies among schools. Formal power is typically given by the principal rather than the Board of Education, although the Board may formally sanction shared governance or "site-based" councils. In advanced shared governance settings, power is assumed to be shared by all, thus equalizing the authority of administrators and teachers, and group decisions are implemented regardless of the principals' personal disposition.

Chairperson—Council members elect a chairperson, who is seldom the principal, except during the early stages of the shared governance initiative.

Principal's Role—The principal is usually a member of the council but is "one among the many" and holds only one vote on issues discussed.

Meetings—Regular (at least quarterly) meetings are held at times convenient for the council members (in some cases consideration for release time is given, as for the annual in-depth planning session of the council). Agendas are distributed to all school personnel, invitations are issued, and regular communications, including minutes of the meetings, are distributed. These meetings are characterized by openness to new ideas, a nonthreatening atmosphere, and problem-solving that uses action research.

Goals—The mission of the shared governance council centers on *instructional improvement*, although significant time may be devoted to structural and administrative matters of concern during the early stages of the initiative. Annual discussion of the goals of the school and regular discussions of matters of import to all school community members take precedence over all other matters.

Support—In varying degrees, time and financial support are available to further the work of the council. Also, members of the council take seriously their charge to provide symbolic forms of support to the school community (e.g., highlighting successful projects, providing professional support and encouragement for challenging projects, and encouraging others to become involved in important issues).

Staff Development—A significant element in successful shared governance initiatives is the presence of major staff development programs. Staff development includes sessions on communication, group development skills, problem solving, decision making, and teacher leadership. During the beginning phases of the initiative, council members may derive such information from other schools or consortia with similar initiatives; less frequently this information is derived from districtwide staff development programs. Teachers usually take an active role in defining and implementing staff development.

Matters of Consideration—In well-developed shared governance initiatives, the focus of the council's deliberations extends beyond technical and managerial matters to schoolwide improvement and instructional matters. In these advanced decision-making situations, critical issues, such as instructional budgeting and hiring of faculty and staff, are included in the responsibilities of council members.

Teacher Effects

Clearly, the impact of principals' leadership on shared governance structures constitutes a powerful and important aspect of teacher empowerment. Some of the major positive effects of principals' leadership on teacher empowerment through the development of shared governance structures are described below.

Teacher Reflection

A primary effect of involvement in formal shared decision-making structures is the *enhancement of teachers' reflective orientation.* We found that teachers become actively involved in considering their actions and the impacts of those actions on student learning and development. They modify their teaching in response to student needs, and they consider the moral and ethical import of their actions. Teachers also develop a *deeper commitment* to become actively involved in dealing with schoolwide problems, as several teachers remarked (all emphases added throughout):

> Our principal set up liaison groups which discuss concerns and interests of the faculty and then provide feedback to the administration. I feel listened to. *I am more likely to think through problems and come up with practical solutions.* I go to meetings with the motivation to get things changed. I am more likely to participate in group deliberation.

> The principal is an excellent delegator of authority. She has assigned one administrator per grade level to communicate with the grade level teachers and back with her. It shows that *she values the classroom teacher's viewpoints* of the "big picture" of school management. Her delegation philosophy makes me feel my input is valid. *I try to think through better solutions* to procedures or problems. I observe more closely the structure or methods being used to bring about a goal.

> He listens to our ideas and acts on them if at all possible. He doesn't ever say "that won't work" and that's it for us. *I think*

about ways to make a better school because I know I will be
heard. I gripe less and am more constructive in my comments
about the school.

She informs the staff of problems before they get out of hand;
it makes me think about how to handle the situation, and I
take action.

He seeks input when a decision is made. Decisions that affect
the school are discussed at faculty meetings and voted on. *I
spend more time thinking* about questions because part of the
responsibility for answers is mine!

Although change theorists advocate systematic approaches to
organizational improvement, the fact of the matter is that such
improvement in schools often is not systematic. In general, our data
suggest that teachers' reflective action in shared governance schools
was a systematic effort consisting of several dimensions: reflection,
planning, implementation, and assessment. Teachers reported that
the following principal leadership behaviors contributed to teachers' capacity for reflection:

- Giving "freedom to think" (opportunity)
- Recognizing the value of thinking
- Expressing confidence in independent thought
- Providing opportunities to implement thinking (e.g., support-
  ing innovative ideas, providing time for planning)
- Granting responsibility for one's thinking/action
- Encouraging sharing, discussion, and debate of ideas

Teacher Motivation

Teachers also reported that greater *motivation*—described by
terms such as "energy," "excitement," "enthusiasm," "drive," and
"inspiration"—resulted from principals' facilitation of shared governance structures:

I feel more enthusiastic toward teaching in knowing that my opinions and goals are valued and important.

I am more motivated because I make a difference in my work environment and receive credit.

I feel empowered through the leadership teams and through the liaison groups in which all concerns are expressed by the faculty and taken to the leadership team for discussion and action.

When my principal empowers me with making schoolwide decisions, I feel she is respecting my professional knowledge and experience. She is listening to me. *We need this reinforcement to motivate the juices* to keep on pumping ideas in our minds.

He has confidence in teachers' abilities. *This confidence motivates me* to plan activities which enhance my teaching. Instead of leading my students to the assigned books, I go beyond to create ways to help them learn and apply their learning.

Increases in teacher motivation were further associated with many ancillary areas of teachers' work:

I have a drive to do more. I want to continue taking risks that will encourage parents [and others] to be part of the school.

She really tries to make everyone feel a part of the decision-making process. What I think about the school counts. This encourages me to go to staff meetings, not just because it is required.

A Sense of Team

Teachers indicated that principals' support for the development of shared governance structures contributed to the teachers' *sense of team.* This refers to their close identification with both school-based shared governance structures and processes as well as with other faculty and school administrators:

> My principal wants her staff to share in decisions affecting teachers and students. *I feel like part of a total team* when given a chance to express my attitude and views.

> He always felt we could handle a problem. We in turn felt we could solve problems of the school. We felt in control and *part of the school.*

> He encourages the faculty to be involved in decision making. We are given many opportunities to make suggestions and vote on issues which affect the running of the school. This makes me feel like a *valuable member* of a working team.

> The staff was always treated with respect and because of that *felt valued as individuals as well as a team.* This makes me feel empowered because I feel a sense of equality with the administration as we work together to achieve a common goal.

Ownership

Our data point out that teachers' sense of ownership, a major aspect of empowerment, resulted from principals' efforts to build school governance structures. "Ownership" refers to teachers' positive identification with and greater responsibility for shared governance structures and processes as well as the outcomes of such structures and processes (e.g., decisions, agreements, policies, and programs), as teachers explained,

> *By expecting us to take responsibility for our school,* the principal *gives me a sense of ownership.* This ownership makes me try to excel and participate in a more rounded way outside of my classroom and in the school.

Delegating out the responsibilities to the staff puts many of the decision-making issues in the hands of the staff. *When the staff feels important and involved they have a sense of ownership* in the overall operation of the school and will contribute in a more positive and enthusiastic way.

Shared decision making makes me feel empowered because it *gives me a sense of ownership* in my school. I am making corporate-like decisions which affect many people but I am trusted to do this.

Our faculty helps to decide how many teachers and aides we will have according to our allotment. When money is available for books and equipment, we get to spend it as we see fit. This makes me feel more important. *It gives me a feeling of ownership in the school.* When our school excels I feel like I deserve part of the credit.

The principal allows discussion and then voting on the part of teachers in liaison groups and the Executive Council to establish policy. *I feel important.* If teachers have a voice in decisions, then they own them and will buy into them.

Commitment

Teachers explained that increases in work commitment were linked to the leadership of shared governance principals. This concept specifically denotes dedication and determination in pursuing educational improvement through group-level and individual-level empowerment. "More involved," "caring," "dedicated," "committed," "invested," and "interested" were words that teachers used to discuss deeper levels of commitment that they identified with their sense of empowerment:

I have *participated* in several meetings in which suggestions for programs, implementation for curriculum . . . have been brought up. Our principal is very open and receptive.

I *feel an investment* in the school and how it deals with the students I teach.

I feel that the mission statement is a large responsibility and a very important part of our school. Being allowed to have a large part in the decision-making process gives me a *feeling of empowerment.* I have a greater interest and involvement in the issues that surround our school.

The principal is very supportive of new ideas and allows teachers to take risks, to try new things and find out if those things, ideas, and methods are successful. This *makes me feel empowered* because I am making decisions in the classroom and with other faculty members. I am more caring and involved with what's going on throughout the school.

Our principal is always open to listening to suggestions and opinions. She encourages risk taking as a natural process of change. I am a *more productive* teacher, a dedicated teacher.

When I receive the opportunity to serve on committees, I feel respected, trusted, and important in the overall school operation. I feel *more committed* and enthusiastic about my professional duties.

Sense of Professionalism

Teacher empowerment was associated with a greater sense of professionalism acquired from working with shared governance principals. Teachers' sense of professionalism referred to seeing oneself as a "trusted" and "respected" individual with the authority and the ability to make independent decisions and to participate responsibly in schoolwide governance processes. This concept was described in terms of a new relationship of "equality" with school administrators: However, in the very early stages of implementation of shared governance structures, teachers felt that involvement in decision making was a gift from the principal instead of a right or responsibility. The following comments from teachers exemplify how they felt about this issue:

> She allowed the teachers to choose committees to participate in and run those committees. *Because I am able to have a say in how I think the schools should function, I feel empowered* within our school. I like being trusted as a professional to make decisions concerning our school. My behavior could be described as *confident*. I feel more *professional* because I am being treated more professionally.

> The staff was always treated with respect and because of that we felt valued as individuals as well as a team. *This makes me feel empowered because I feel a sense of equality* with the administration as we work together to achieve a common goal. I am a professional.

> Trust. My principal allows me to do my job without day-to-day involvement by him. *This trust makes me feel empowered because major decisions about my area of expertise are made by me.* I behave in a professional manner because my principal's behavior demonstrates the trust he places in me.

> My principal has a professional attitude toward teaching. She treats her staff as equals and listens when they need to express thoughts and feelings about their jobs. She makes herself available to teachers and others as often as possible at school and by phone. When I am treated as an equal, I feel better about my job and have feelings of professionalism. *When I am treated as a professional I act professionally.*

A Cautionary Note

Although principals' implementation of shared governance structures usually influenced teachers' sense of empowerment in a positive way, a few teachers, in describing one principal's indecisiveness that led to "inefficiency" and "uncertainty," reported experiencing feelings of frustration. This was not the normal anxiety that invariably accompanies organizational change efforts (and which is usually diminished by a confident, secure principal who holds tenaciously to the tenets of shared governance even as some cynics resist). In this case, indecisiveness about decision-making procedures and teachers' roles in the governance of the school led to confusion and frustration. In another instance, feelings of anger were apparent in reports about a principal who engaged in actions that two teachers believed contradicted shared governance tenets. One teacher commented,

> Our principal might have given us the freedom to choose, select, and be part of the school-wide governing process, but I never felt "empowered." I always felt that our principal expected a great deal from us and the pressure was great to work 110% all the time. I felt "powered by" instead of a sense of empowerment.

Participation and delegation should not be tools to compensate for the weaknesses of incompetent administrators, nor should they be insincere offers of involvement by power-hungry administrators. Rather, participation and delegation must be *authentic* points of collaboration through which principals realize some of the advantages of shared governance (e.g., *better* decisions). Our study indicates that successful shared governance principals *need* genuine faculty and staff involvement to create more effective schools.

We also note that principals will inevitably encounter some difficulty as teachers realize that shared decision making is not a panacea: It does not ensure that things always "go your way," it takes more time to enact by virtue of the number of people involved, and it cannot solve all of a school's problems.

Tips for Initiating Shared Governance Structures: A Baker's Dozen

On the basis of our teachers' reports, we offer the following 13 suggestions, or "best practices," for initiating shared governance structures and empowering teachers. Keep in mind the special and unique context of your school as you proceed.

1. Assess your faculty and staff's readiness.

Before initiating a shared governance approach in your school, consider implementability, assess your own strengths for leading in a participative decision-making climate, determine the concerns and potential levels of use of a shared governance approach by personnel, and consider the level of collegial interactions among faculty and staff. Consideration of these factors will provide benchmarks of readiness to engage in shared governance.

2. Actively participate as an equal.

In an effective shared governance initiative the principal is deeply involved as an *equal participant*, not as a superior, in the decisions made by the council. This means that the principal sits with the council during meetings, has one (and *only* one) vote each time a decision is made, and may even choose to participate on committees or task forces. Even though it may be difficult to completely "shed the stripes of authority and hierarchy," a principal's need for control can eventually be translated into trust in others (Bredeson, 1989, p. 20). One principal commented that she remained as silent as possible *in the early stages of shared governance* because "it takes a long time for teachers to *not* put too much emphasis on the principal's comments." Teachers themselves were more frequently able to bring up points for consideration.

3. Be enthusiastic.

Remember that enthusiasm is contagious! As one teacher said about the principal, "He has pursued the formation of this shared governance body with *vigor, enthusiasm!*" Your spirited demonstration of sincere *support* for a shared governance initiative forms an irresistible foundation on which to build a strong professional alliance as colleagues and team members.

4. Ensure inclusion.

All faculty and staff members should be included in school-based decision making. Paraprofessionals, secretaries, and other support staff members are essential to the effective functioning of the school, and they provide significant services for students. Excluding them from discussions and decisions about the school amounts to treating them as unimportant—an untenable and offensive assumption. Encourage everyone to participate and help in decision making about your school. One teacher in our study related this incident:

> Once when I was absent [from a meeting] and missed a vote on an issue, [the principal] made a point of contacting me the next day with the assurance that if my vote would have decided things either way, she would have waited until I could vote.

As noted earlier, *parents* were also active members of the decision-making structures in the advanced shared governance projects. Finally, remember that inclusion guarantees dissent, which must be welcomed and explored.

5. Provide opportunities to meet.

Principals must provide *adequate time* for the council and committees to meet on a regular basis. The work of a collegial team of educators who share the governance of a school must take place when members *can be present* without having to miss other important activities and when they can seriously concentrate on matters at hand. With a little creativity and coordination, such meetings can occur at routinely scheduled times and not during "tired time" right after long, hard days at work. Strive to make this possible; results will undoubtedly reflect your efforts.

6. Be flexible.

The formal shared governance design that you and the faculty/ staff initiate in your school may, on occasion, prove too rigid or inadequate to meet current needs. Consider compensating for this by *opening up your procedures* and *experimenting* with new structures; it may prove beneficial. Ad hoc committees, for example, might be a useful way to encourage the participation of small groups of teachers who are intensely interested in a particular project not subsumed by the responsibilities of standing or formal committees.

7. Support voluntary participation.

Individuals must be free to *select committees, teams, or groups of interest* for membership. Along with responsibility comes the need for freedom to choose how and when one participates. This eliminates the need to assign people to work that does not interest them, work that is often consciously or unconsciously sabotaged by unwilling participants. Have faith that teachers will fulfill their professional responsibilities.

8. Build trust.

As discussed in Chapter 2, trust is the foundation of all collaborative efforts. Being a *model of trustworthiness* yourself (e.g., being open, fair, consistent, honest, and supportive) will yield great returns in collegial problem-solving efforts. Above all, win-lose situations must be avoided; whenever possible, educators should try to reach *consensus* rather than putting an issue to a vote. In attaining consensus, all persons' opinions are *heard, considered, and respected*; hence one is willing to support the collective decision even if different from one's own view.

9. Protect the integrity of decisions and surrender power.

Except in cases of legal imperatives or policy limitations, principals must refrain from all actions that contradict a committee's decisional authority once that authority has been granted. Although teachers want and often ask for advice from principals during deliberations, it is a mistake for principals to monitor and second-guess decisions or to impose their preferences. Urge teachers to take responsibility, give them opportunities to make decisions, remind them that they too are educational leaders, and share your own ideas for consideration just as any other participant does. As one teacher put it, "The principal does not solve problems or settle conflicts; she gives *encouragement.*"

10. Encourage a team spirit.

"Collaboration" and "mutuality" are words that teachers in our study used to describe the fundamental character of their shared governance schools. This view must be felt by teachers, support staff, and administrators. One way to put it might be "one for all and all for one!" Shor and Freire (1987) have argued that there is no personal self-empowerment for teachers; empowerment is always a social act worked out among people, given the complexity of teachers' situation.

11. Support risk.

Support of risk is discussed in greater detail in Chapters 5 and 7. For now, suffice it to say that the successful shared governance principal is *comfortable with experimentation* and knows that *innovation and improvement require risk taking on the part of teachers.*

12. Encourage a problem-solving approach.

Being available to help in problem-solving efforts, encouraging and listening to individual input, and *structuring* daily operations so as to support team-oriented problem solving are essential to shared governance efforts (see Chapter 9 for a detailed discussion of successful shared governance principals' efforts along these lines).

13. Dare to challenge the status quo.

The specific strategies used by effective shared governance principals to support participative decision making invariably produce some resistance by a small percentage of teachers. Cynicism often abounds among those who find any substantial change threatening. Yet the teachers in our study who witnessed such negativity disclosed that their principals *held firm to the ideals and tenets of shared governance* in the face of adversity. Teachers also reported strong positive feelings of respect and admiration for these principals.

References

Barth, R. S. (1988). School: A community of leaders. In A. Lieberman (Ed.), *Building a professional culture in schools* (pp. 129-147). New York: Teachers College Press.

Bird, T., & Little, J. W. (1986). How schools organize the teaching occupation. *Elementary School Journal, 86,* 495-511.

Bolin, F. S. (1989). Empowering leadership. *Teachers College Record, 91,* 81-96.

Bredeson, P. V. (1989). Redefining leadership and the roles of school principals: Responses to changes in the professional worklife of teachers. *The High School Journal, 73*(1), 9-20.

Flinders, D. J. (1988). Teacher isolation and the new reform. *Journal of Curriculum and Supervision, 4,* 17-29.

Glickman, C. D. (1993). *Renewing America's schools: A guide for school-based action.* San Francisco: Jossey-Bass.

Glickman, C. D., & Allen, L. (Eds.). (1992-1993). *The league of professional schools: Lessons from the field* (Vols. 1-2). Athens: University of Georgia, Program for School Improvement.

Goodlad, J. (1984). *A place called school: Prospects for the future.* New York: McGraw-Hill.

Greene, M. (1988). *The dialectic of freedom.* New York: Teachers College Press.

Hall, G. E., & Hord, S. M. (1984). Analyzing what change facilitators do. *Knowledge: Creation, Diffusion, Utilization, 5*(3), 275-307.

Hall, G. E., Loucks, S. F., Rutherford, W. L., & Newlove, B. (1975). Levels of use of the innovation: A framework for analyzing innovation adoption. *Journal of Teacher Education, 24,* 52-56.

Hall, G. E., Wallace, R. C., Jr., & Dorsett, W. A. (1973). *A developmental conceptualization of the adoption process within educational institutions.* Austin: University of Texas, Research and Development Center for Teacher Education.

Hallinger, P., & Richardson, D. (1988). Models of shared leadership: Evolving structures and relationships. *Urban Review, 20*(4), 229-245.

Joyce, B. (1986). *Improving America's schools.* New York: Longman.

Little, J. W. (1987). Teachers as colleagues. In V. Richardson-Koehler (Ed.), *Educator's handbook: A research perspective* (pp. 491-518). New York: Longman.

Lovell, J. T., & Wiles, K. (1983). *Supervision for better schools* (5th ed.). Englewood Cliffs, NJ: Prentice Hall.

Maeroff, G. I. (1988a). A blueprint for empowering teachers. *Phi Delta Kappan, 69,* 473-477.

Maeroff, G. I. (1988b). *The empowerment of teachers: Overcoming the crisis of confidence.* New York: Teachers College Press.

McNeil, L. M. (1988). *Contradictions of control: School structure and school knowledge.* London: Routledge & Kegan Paul.

Roberts, J. (1991, April). *School personnel and improvement projects: Indicators of readiness.* Paper presented at the annual meeting of the American Educational Research Association, Chicago.

Schön, D. A. (1987). *Educating the reflective practitioner: Toward a new design for teaching and learning in the professions.* San Francisco: Jossey-Bass.

Shor, I., & Freire, P. (1987). *A pedagogy for liberation: Dialogues on transforming education.* South Hadley, MA: Bergin & Garvey.

Sizer, T. R. (1984). *Horace's compromise: The dilemma of the American high school.* Boston: Houghton Mifflin.

Strike, K. A. (1993). Professionalism, democracy, and discursive communities: Normative reflections on restructuring. *American Educational and Research Journal, 30*(2), 255-275.

4

A Cornucopia of Supportive Resources

I feel that our principal views my growth and participation as important and that it will result in an improved system. She encourages me to reach my professional potential by making attendance or presenting at professional conferences possible, and she acknowledges involvement. Also, she has recommended me for awards. I feel valued and appreciated.

—Middle School Teacher

Staff development can be a powerful tool for improvement in classroom instruction. But it can be much more. It can form the foundation for teacher growth and collegial support that results in new, more authentic approaches to teaching and learning. Research has shown that a significant amount of internal assistance (e.g., training, consulting, coordination, and capacity building) is crucial to implementing successful school reform projects (Louis & Miles, 1990).

So it is in shared governance schools: A strong commitment to invest in various forms of teacher development must exist. Little (1993), when she noted the "uneven fit" between current models of professional development and reform efforts (e.g., the dominance of a training approach as opposed to an inquiry, problem-solving, and knowledge production approach), concluded the following:

> Much staff development or inservice communicates a relatively impoverished view of teachers, teaching, and teacher development. Compared with the complexity, subtlety, and uncertainties of the classroom, professional development is often a remarkably low-intensity enterprise. It requires little in the way of intellectual struggle or emotional engagement and takes only superficial account of teachers' histories or circumstances. Compared with the complexity and ambiguity of the most ambitious reforms, professional development is too often substantively weak and politically marginal.
>
> Professional development must be constructed in ways that deepen the discussion, open up the debates, and enrich the array of possibilities for action. (p. 148)

In one Rhode Island school restructuring program (Rallis, 1990), teacher-principal cadres were first trained in team approaches to problem-solving and group process strategies. Time, space, and resources were managed so that teachers could collaborate to identify problems and create solutions as well as to set and act on their own agendas. The principal had *created an atmosphere* that symbolically, politically, and structurally enabled the teachers to act and grow professionally, and they did. Indeed, if teachers are empowered and if they take the education of students seriously, most will become increasingly concerned about instructional issues and will work toward improving practice (Bolin, 1989).

One of the best forums for instructional improvement is in collaboration or cooperative learning among groups of teachers. Cooperative approaches have an excellent chance of yielding high achievement, positive relationships, and psychologically healthy people (Johnson & Johnson, 1989). In contrast to individual approaches to learning, collaborative approaches provide access to more relevant information and alternative perspectives, promote reflective practice, help develop a culture that supports learning and growth, and facilitate change by virtue of the encouragement and validation of changes that occur (Osterman & Kottkamp, 1993). The principal's role is that of a *facilitator who enables others* to enter a reflective conversation about teaching and learning (Schön, 1983) rather than that of an educator who "start[s] with knowledge already organized and proceed[s] to ladle it out in doses" (Dewey, 1938, p. 82).

Recent studies of teachers (Petrie, 1989) and principals (Anderson & Page, in press) have added to our understanding of the phenomenon of reflective practice; these studies have described practitioners' epistemologies of practice according to the *kinds of knowledge* they use. From such work we have begun to realize the importance of supporting extended opportunities for teachers to share "deep narratives" of their practical knowledge (i.e., discuss their technical, local, craft, and personal knowledge). This can be done through a process of uncovering and analyzing the "invisible frames" or subtle norms that legitimate, perpetuate, and even restrict educational practices and teacher-to-teacher discussions. In this way, the powerful assumptions and themes driving current school reform efforts can be made explicit and held up for scrutiny. This approach can foster the process of "critical knowledge" and bring new perspectives to bear on problems of practice.

Liston and Zeichner (1991) have advocated a "social reconstructionist" approach to teacher education programs. This approach incorporates critical reflection, journaling, and practical inquiry: Discussions among teachers are based on both the structure of programs or their prescribed content *and the narrativity (talks) of experience around the knowledge base that teachers possess.* In sum, *dialogue and critical reflection* promote the empowerment of teachers and democratic schools; the shared governance principal's role becomes one of communicating, coordinating, mutual problem solving, and providing resources for effective work.

Guiding Assumptions

Osterman and Kottkamp (1993) have contrasted the traditional model of teaching with the reflective practice model of professional development. The former is characterized by such notions as instructor as expert; learner as subordinate; and individual, molecular, cognitive learning processes. The latter emphasizes the instructor as facilitator, learners as agents, and collaborative, holistic, and personal approaches to professional development.

From our study we learned that effective shared governance principals held certain assumptions about the nature of staff development that parallel the reflective model of teaching identified above. The following assumptions seemed to guide their efforts and plans to help teachers grow:

1. The principal is a *guide or facilitator* for staff development.

Principals described in our study concentrated their efforts on enabling teachers to work together by providing time and resources for professional development. These principals also ensured that faculty (and staff) members collaborated to determine school goals and ways to work toward them. A powerful message is sent to teachers, who are expected to assume responsibility for their own development.

2. *Everyone* can improve.

Just as teachers must believe that all students can learn, given time and opportunity, shared governance principals believe that all professionals can learn more about their craft and improve in their ability to deliver top-quality instruction and learning opportunities for students. The administrators in shared governance schools also learn, side by side with the teachers, new ways of working together and individually for the benefit of the students.

3. Change comes from *realizing that something is not quite right* or not as good as it could be.

Basing their decisions on data about student knowledge, attitudes, and skills, principals work to encourage teachers to fill gaps, provide better programs, and upgrade their own skills.

4. *Change is challenging and emotional.*

Changing the ways administrators and teachers work together and the ways teachers teach can be complex and demanding. Often, this taxes individuals as they struggle to attain new skills. Successful shared governance principals model support and encouragement for those who are working to create a better program, and they apply what they have learned about the process of change to improvement efforts.

5. Teachers can *teach each other.*

Cooperative learning is not just for students. Shared governance principals encourage teachers to tap their considerable professional expertise and routinely share their knowledge with one another. They support teachers in their efforts to be responsible for the design and implementation of training sessions as well as the follow-up programs that enable them to translate newly acquired knowledge into action in the classroom.

6. Staff development will take *many forms.*

Shared governance principals make available a variety of learning experiences to teachers. One might see, for example, teachers learning in pairs or small groups (see Joyce & Showers, 1988, for a discussion of the methods and value of *coaching* for teacher development). There might also be role-playing, talking and sharing, centers of study and activity, and cooperative learning activities. What is key is the *variety* of learning opportunities, appropriate to the situation and context, which provide information that can be applied to the problems of practice.

7. All educators engage in *action research.*

Shared governance principals believe that action research should inform the decisions made by teachers to improve their school. Gathering and sharing information about the results of one's performance motivates teachers to improve. As Schön (1983) said, "When a practitioner becomes a researcher into his [her] own practice, [s]he engages in a continuing process of self-education" (p. 299). Both principals and teachers need training and support in the collection and analysis of data to help clarify goals, determine procedures, and study progress via-à-vis students, teachers, administrators, parents, and other community members (see Calhoun, 1991, and Joyce, Wolf, & Calhoun, 1993, for suggestions on how to collect, analyze, and use data for school improvement).

The Principal's Role

In a study of the principal's role in forging new relationships with classroom teachers, Bredeson (1989) found that in schools with empowered teachers the principals supported and positively affected the teachers' professional work by the following methods:

- Providing time, space, and money to implement ideas
- Reassuring people that ideas and plans, even when challenged, are valued
- Letting go throughout the growth process (not directing others, staying out of the way, and allowing mistakes)
- Being informed
- Being available
- Providing an open, friendly, supportive environment

Bredeson also reported that principals did *not* convey a "know it all" attitude and did not judge others. Instead, they modeled an acceptance of problems as opportunities for improvement.

Argyris and Schön's (1974) Model II, an action theory that explains beliefs about people and their motivation, suggests that openly sharing information can improve the quality of interpersonal relations, stimulate professional growth, and enhance organizational effectiveness. Research has consistently confirmed that the Model II theory-in-use encourages trust, collaboration, and effective problem solving (Blase & Kirby, 1992; Leithwood & Jantzi, 1990; Parkay & Hall, 1992). Indeed, open communication and sharing appear to be the foundation for collaborative work on school improvement.

Our data indicate that successful shared governance principals realize that teachers require help in enhancing their professional knowledge and skills. Similar to the effective traditional principals described in Blase and Kirby's (1992) study, *Bringing Out the Best in Teachers*, the principals in our study used considerable caution and diplomacy in their attempts to improve instruction through staff development activities. They respected teachers' need for autonomy and professionalism in choosing to involve themselves in professional growth activities. They seemed to recognize both the need to differentiate among teachers' needs (Bacharach, Conley, & Shedd, 1986) and the need to diagnose the social context of the school (Blake & Mouton, 1985; Hersey & Blanchard, 1982). The shared governance principals described in our study possessed a *repertoire* of staff development responses, which we call "strategic support."

Strategic Support

Shared governance principals use several strategies to increase teacher knowledge. They provide opportunities for professional development, current professional literature, and additional support in the form of basic resources when possible. They also make themselves available to teachers to talk and share thoughts about teaching.

Professional Development

Principals provided formal staff development opportunities on a variety of topics to facilitate schoolwide educational improvement and teachers' professional growth. In shared governance schools, teachers often participated in *initiating* and *defining* staff development activities, and we found that this involvement enhanced their sense of empowerment. Even when principals took the initiative in defining topics for staff development, their decisions were generally *congruent* with teachers' needs, values, and goals. Principals also were willing to make available consultative services for work with teachers. Several teachers' comments about their principals' approach to professional development opportunities are presented below:

She provides and encourages opportunities for growth.

Staff development is determined by staff members.

I was given the opportunity to visit other schools and enquire about new instructional programs being used.

He brings in speakers to tell us about ideas relevant to our needs.

[She considers] the totality of the institution. She considers ancillary areas in relating the information necessary to provide an appropriate educational environment for both students and staff. She requested resource personnel to conduct an inservice for teams, giving them information they didn't have and then offering educational options not previously considered.

One highly effective approach to staff development used by one of the authors involves 20-minute minisessions in which staff members (or representatives from liaison groups) learn about and practice group development skills (communication, decision making, trust building, conflict, leadership, dealing with change). The effect is immediate and powerful; participants apply their learning to everyday situations and generalize to other possible scenarios (for a sampling of such minisessions, see Roberts, 1991).

Professional Literature

To encourage innovation and professional growth among teachers (two aspects of empowerment), principals provided teachers with relevant professional articles and information about professional conferences and workshops. Regarding the latter, one teacher commented,

The characteristic of my principal which contributes to empowerment is his ability to seek out new ideas to share with his staff. Our principal always keeps us informed about new educational improvements and invites us to attend various workshops. I am constantly finding flyers from different conferences in my mailbox along with articles relating to educational reform.

Additional Support

Our study suggests that shared governance principals provide supportive basic resources in a timely fashion to encourage teacher growth. For example, principals acted on their own initiative and responded to teachers' requests in providing resources such as *time*. One teacher noted, "She has time set aside for 6 weeks planning for each grade level."

Shared governance principals also provided *educational materials* and financial resources needed by teachers:

My principal does not dictate. He asks "What do you think about whole language?" or "What materials do you need to be a better teacher or teach a better unit?"

In dealing with a relatively new program my principal is desirous of helping me make it a success through major support—both financial and other. I am given the responsibility to make it work and to make choices which will accomplish this. I feel supported and important to the school.

Availability

Successful shared governance principals consistently made themselves available to discuss instructional or related matters with teachers and to deal with professional problems identified by teachers. One teacher remarked,

He is always available at approximately 7:00 a.m. each morning. His office door is open and he makes time for me. Questions are answered, problems are discussed, suggestions are exchanged.

Some shared governance principals even made themselves available to teachers during after-school hours. In the teachers' view, the principals' open-mindedness, fairness, willingness to provide advice, and respect for and confidence in teachers' judgments facilitated their ability to deal with school-related problems (for more about problem solving, see Chapter 9).

Impacts From Support

By providing staff development, professional literature, additional basic resources, and time and openness for discussion, shared governance principals afforded important strategic support for teachers' work and enhanced their sense of empowerment. First, teachers reported that their principals' support for staff development affected their feelings of *confidence* and their inclination toward trying *innovative and creative classroom instruction*. Impacts on teachers' classroom *efficacy* as well as on *motivation and esteem* were derived from the use of the professional literature and support to attend professional conferences. Making oneself available for collaborative problem solving had strong impacts on *satisfaction, motivation, confidence*, and *security*—all of which are associated with empowerment. Finally, providing basic resources such as time and materials had impacts on feelings of *inclusion*. Clearly, the cornucopia of supportive resources provided by shared governance principals reflects a commitment to teacher development and an investment in the educational program provided for students.

Implications for Practice

We cannot suggest the *best* staff development activities or the *right* programs and literature to use; all such support must be appropriate to the context of the school and the needs of the faculty/staff. On the basis of our findings, however, we can present several suggestions for implementing professional growth programs for teachers.

1. **Relate all staff development activities to the school's "driving dream."**

Keep the clear, shared vision, or "driving dream," in sight; this will support change efforts, help to articulate values, and supply direction for your developmental work (Miles & Ekholm, 1991).

2. Provide a variety of staff development opportunities.

Teacher growth is facilitated by a variety of staff development activities. Be open to paired or small-group explorations, role-playing, cooperative learning activities, centers of inquiry, and any other creative methods that allow teachers to experiment and learn new skills.

3. Respect teachers' judgments about implementation.

Encourage teachers' use and evaluation of new methods and acknowledge their expert judgment about the merits of new approaches. Teachers, more than any other persons in the educational setting, are knowledgeable and wise about student needs and abilities.

4. Be knowledgeable.

Principals must obtain current knowledge of curricular and instructional trends. You can help teachers improve by disseminating excellent professional materials that provide clear, concrete suggestions for classroom use.

5. Strive for institutionalization of staff development activities.

Staff development activities should be built in, embedded in the work of the school. A regular budget, annual schedule, and job responsibilities must be designated so as to move from implementation to institutionalization.

6. Avoid staleness.

It is ironic that new structures become boring or spiceless as they become institutionalized. Along with the idea of having teachers design and conduct staff development activities Miles and Ekholm

(1991) offer several suggestions for maintaining interest and commitment after high-energy days have passed: (a) maintain continuous critical examination of new structures, (b) reward "lively and humorous" uses, (c) rotate responsibilities, and (d) protect alternative structures to maintain variety as well as the allegiance of resisters.

References

Anderson, G. L., & Page, B. (in press). Narrative knowledge and educational administration: The stories that guide our practice. In R. Donmoyer, M. Imber, & J. Scheurich (Eds.), *The knowledge base in educational administration: Multiple perspectives*. Albany: State University of New York Press.

Argyris, C., & Schön, D. A. (1974). *Theory in practice: Increasing professional effectiveness*. San Francisco: Jossey-Bass.

Bacharach, S. B., Conley, S., & Shedd, J. (1986). Beyond career ladders: Structuring teacher career development systems. *Teachers College Record, 87*(4), 563-574.

Blake, R. R., & Mouton, J. S. (1985). *The managerial grid, III*. Houston, TX: Gulf.

Blase, J., & Kirby, P. C. (1992). *Bringing out the best in teachers: What effective principals do*. Newbury Park, CA: Corwin.

Bolin, F. S. (1989). Empowering leadership. *Teachers College Record, 91*(1), 81-96.

Bredeson, P. V. (1989). Redefining leadership and the roles of school principals: Responses to changes in the professional worklife of teachers. *The High School Journal, 73*(1), 9-20.

Calhoun, E. (1991, April). *A wide-angle lens: How to increase the variety, collection, and use of data for school improvement*. Paper presented at the annual meeting of the American Educational Research Association, Chicago.

Dewey, J. (1938). *Experience and education*. New York: Macmillan.

Hersey, P., & Blanchard, K. G. (1982). *Management of organizational behavior: Utilizing human resources* (4th ed.). Englewood Cliffs, NJ: Prentice Hall.

Johnson, D. W., & Johnson, R. (1989). *Cooperation and competition: Theory and research*. Edina, MN: Interaction Book Company.

Joyce, B., & Showers, B. (1988). *Student achievement through staff development*. New York: Longman.

Joyce, B., Wolf, J., & Calhoun, E. (1993). *The self-renewing school*. Alexandria, VA: Association for Supervision and Curriculum Development.

Leithwood, K., & Jantzi, D. (1990, April). *Transformational leadership: How principals can help reform school cultures*. Paper presented at the annual meeting of the American Educational Research Association, Boston.

Liston, D., & Zeichner, K. (1991). *Teacher education and the social conditions of schooling*. New York: Routledge.

Little, J. W. (1993). Teachers' professional development in a climate of educational reform. *Educational Evaluation and Policy Analysis, 15*(2), 129-151.

Louis, K. S., & Miles, M. B. (1990). *Improving the urban high school: What works and why*. New York: Teachers College Press.

Miles, M. B., & Ekholm, M. (1991, April). *Will new structures stay restructured?* Paper presented at the annual meeting of the American Educational Research Association, Chicago.

Osterman, K. F., & Kottkamp, R. B. (1993). *Reflective practice for educators*. Newbury Park, CA: Corwin.

Parkay, F. W., & Hall, G. E. (1992). *Becoming a principal: The challenges of beginning leadership*. Needham Heights, MA: Allyn & Bacon.

Petrie, H. (1989, April). *Teacher knowledge and teacher practice: A new view*. Paper presented at the annual meeting of the American Educational Research Association, San Francisco.

Rallis, S. F. (1990, April). *Teachers and organizational change: Can professionalism transform schools?* Paper presented at the annual meeting of the American Educational Research Association, Boston.

Roberts, J. (1991). *How to reduce conflict, how to improve communication, and how to teach problem-solving skills* (Tips for Principals Series). Reston, VA: National Association of Secondary School Principals.

Schön, D. A. (1983). *The reflective practitioner: How professionals think in action*. New York: Basic Books.

5

Encouraging Autonomy and Innovation

Teachers are *praised* for innovative teaching. When I discover a new idea or strategy I feel free to try this out in my class. Even when this doesn't work I will be encouraged to learn from the experience and to try again. I try many new things I might otherwise shy away from.

—Middle School Teacher

Even the most expert teachers have difficulty describing what it is exactly that they do to provide superb learning opportunities for their students. Yet the inability to describe their own brilliant strategies is common to experts in many fields. Berliner (1986) found that the intellectual and technical qualities exhibited by master teachers were equivalent to those exhibited by experts in such areas as chess, surgery, athletics, or aviation. Besides such intellectual and technical knowledge, there are moral, social, and political qualities in teaching that have been delineated by educators and philosophers such as Maxine Greene and Henry Giroux; these qualities are undeniably human and *necessary* to the craft of teaching. Goodlad, Soder, and Sirotnik (1990) have declared that education is a *special* profession, one with complex cognitive, social, political, and moral demands. A wealth of new literature in which teachers describe their work (see, e.g., Bredemeier, 1988; Kidder, 1989; Wigginton, 1985) provides glimpses of the complex nature of this challenging profession.

71

What can principals do to support and encourage teachers in their ability to handle the complex human contingencies that comprise teaching? How can principals unlock the potential and confidence of teachers? What can they do to help teachers respond to the ambiguity and indeterminism that always accompany teaching and learning and to deal with the risks taken in the name of instructional improvement? Finally, how can principals support teachers' work related to students' intellectual and social development and achievement (Blase & Greenfield, 1981; Lortie, 1975; Mitchell, Ortiz, & Mitchell, 1987) while also striving to achieve integration, collegiality, and collaboration (conditions of work that are often contrary to teachers' culture)?

Teachers in our study explained that two strategies used by shared governance principals—encouraging teacher autonomy and encouraging teacher innovation—were primary factors in enabling them to release their instructional potential. In the context of our data, *autonomy* refers to the degree of freedom that teachers have in determining their work processes, and *innovation* refers to the design and implementation of experimental processes and new content for use in the classroom. Lack of intrusion—that is, *freedom from* intrusion —and wide discretion in instructional matters—that is, *freedom to* determine one's own course (Rosenholtz, 1989)—have been linked with principal effectiveness elsewhere (Blase & Kirby, 1992). In this chapter we describe shared governance principals' strategies of encouraging teacher autonomy and innovation and the effects of those strategies on the teachers' sense of empowerment.

Empowering Teachers
by Encouraging Autonomy

Shared governance principals demonstrated great interest in promoting individual teacher decisional authority, or autonomy, primarily in classroom instructional and student control matters. Levels of autonomy varied among the schools we studied, but in many of these schools teachers exercised what they called *full* autonomy in the classroom.

Such autonomy, according to our findings, has three primary characteristics:

1. Teachers are largely in control of instructional areas of classroom life (e.g., teachers determined the risks they were willing to assume in curriculum and instructional innovations).
2. Teachers generally control noninstructional areas of classroom life (such as disciplinary matters).
3. Teachers determine needs for and access to additional but necessary supplies and materials.

Principals actively encouraged teacher autonomy even when they directly solicited teachers' advice about decisions they made unilaterally because of legal/policy considerations. Teachers frequently described these facets of classroom autonomy in rhapsodic terms (all emphases added throughout):

[The principal] *guides rather than dictates.* She allows teachers to realize their choices. She may explain her reasons for preferring one choice over another, but the choice is usually ultimately left to the teacher.

He trusts me to make the right teaching decisions for my class. I am in control of the order, rate, and amount of time spent on each subject. I don't feel ashamed if I don't follow my lesson plans to the letter. He trusts me to make adjustments as needed.

My principal *listens and encourages me* to go with an idea that I bring to her. Recently, I suggested an alternative assessment project. Not only did she encourage me, but she provided additional materials for me.

Shared governance principals actively *buffered* instructional time from interruptions, thus demonstrating the priority placed on teaching and learning; this protection has been correlated in other studies with teacher discretion and autonomy (Heck, Larsen, & Marcoulides,

1990; Rosenholtz, 1989). Teachers usually defined major limitations on autonomy in shared governance schools as "necessary parameters": district-defined and official syllabi and curricula; standing school policies and rules; faculty and committee decisions; and the principal's (judiciously rendered) salient expectations, advice, and guidance.

Interestingly, there was no indication that teachers in any of the schools in our study felt frustrated with their level of classroom discretion; in fact, they characterized their school climates as "nonthreatening," "supportive," and "reinforcing." The data suggest that, in part, the teachers' satisfaction with their current level of autonomy was shaped by the apparent contrasts in leadership between shared governance principals and the traditional principals *for whom they had worked in the past.* Such principals were often described as "dictatorial," "closed," and "authoritarian."

Possibly the inherently "loosely coupled" nature of schools, in which classroom activity and administrative structures are often weakly connected, did not permit teachers sufficient functional autonomy (Rosenholtz, 1989; Weick, 1976). Teachers explained that in these oppressive circumstances, their principals worked to *control* them rather than to empower them. Teachers described the sharp contrasts between control-oriented and shared governance principals:

> My [current] principal feels and gives the attitude that I am in control of my room. He generates a *sense of management rather than control.*

> I feel like I have control in my classroom. I feel like I can try new activities in the classroom without causing a problem with my principal. In the past, I have felt like *my job was to keep my students silent and busy.*

> [My principal] allows me to make my own rules for my classroom and how my students should be disciplined during class time. In other schools I have taught in, the principal *didn't give you much freedom* on your class rules or your discipline procedures.

Teachers' "new level" of authority over classroom matters, in contrast to their former experiences, enabled them to have the security of being "in control" of their classes. This appears to be one significant element at the heart of teacher empowerment.

Empowering Teachers by Encouraging Innovation

Besides encouraging teacher autonomy in the classroom, one of the most frequently reported principal strategies used to empower teachers was the encouragement of innovation in the classroom. Respondents in our study used terms such as "innovation," "creativity," and "risk taking" to convey what they meant by this type of encouragement. Specifically, principals encouraged teachers to experiment with new teaching techniques, new materials, new curricula, and new programs to improve student learning (see also Chapter 4 for related forms of support). Moreover, although the principals' encouragement of innovation was often directed toward the individual classroom teachers, teams or groups of teachers were also encouraged to work together to provide innovative instruction:

> The principal is very *receptive* to new ideas and ways of doing things. She *values the opinions* of all her staff members. She realizes that our school and our students are unique and welcomes suggestions and ideas for improving instruction. We have an instructional task force that continually teaches new methods of instruction and we are encouraged to try new techniques.

> The principal conveys a *deep sense of trust* in my personal and professional judgment. These responses are genuine, not offhanded, and through them I sense a willingness on her part to assign decision making to me.

By permitting and actively encouraging teachers to go beyond the standard or official curriculum—and to do so without the risks and anxieties that typically accompany innovation and occasional failure—principals helped teachers to be always vigilant for new ideas and new ways to improve instruction. Once again, the data indicate that creating a nonthreatening environment free from fear, criticism, and reprisals for failure was especially important (see Chapter 7 for more about *risk* and *threat*), as evidenced in the following comments:

> Our principal gave permission to try new things. *Risk taking was encouraged* with the understanding that the responsibility came with it. If a teacher was trying cooperative learning for the first time she was not expected to do it perfectly.

> My principal recognizes that there is more than one way to do things; it is possible to *try new things without fear or criticism.* Until there is substantial cause for worry he will not intervene.

When teachers engaged in experimentation and met the occasional but inevitable failure, their principals helped them view the situation as an opportunity to learn important things about their work with students. Principals avoided "blaming" anyone, behaved as colearners, and emphasized positive elements inherent in the less-than-successful efforts. One teacher reported,

> My principal helps me keep my attitude positive. When something goes wrong he tends to look at it as a *learning experience* and finds something positive out of it. I believe it would be impossible to be empowered if you did not have a positive attitude and someone to contribute to this attitude.

The Benefits of Treating
Teachers as Professionals

Granting professional autonomy and supporting teacher innovation are decidedly beneficial to teachers. They indicated that the autonomy and freedom to be innovative significantly enhanced their self-esteem, confidence, professional satisfaction, creativity, sense of classroom efficacy, and ability to reflect on instructional issues:

> He allows teachers to plan activities to extend the curriculum. This *confidence motivates me* to plan activities which enhance my teaching. I perform better and seek to improve my performance as a teacher.

> Recently I suggested an alternative . . . and she encouraged me. If she had faith in me, *it was important for me to do well.*

> Our principal is idealistic. He *embraces new ideas* that others would shy away from. An idealistic principal gives me a license to dream about the way it should be. I behave more creatively.

> Our principal's positive attitude empowers one to try new and exciting teaching strategies. If these strategies are not successful, I am confident that my principal will *thank me for trying* and *reinforce the positive aspects* of the experience. This positive attitude is a constant incentive to continue to try new ideas and teaching strategies.

> [Our principal] *encourages us to use new methods* in the classroom and asks our input on their effectiveness. I feel like I have a say in what's being done schoolwide. [This results in] pride in choices and decisions.

Most of the teachers we studied felt strongly that autonomy in the classroom should be a *right* of professional teachers. However, they realized that in their schools such autonomy was contingent on the principals' goodwill, trust, and confidence in teachers' professional judgment. Although teachers were sensitive to principals' occasional difficulties and in balancing shared decision making with legal duties and responsibilities, they reported that their principals consistently demonstrated great faith in them and valued them as experts and professionals.

Strategies for Promoting
Autonomy and Innovation

Successful shared governance principals encourage teachers to use professional discretion in making decisions in their classrooms while at the same time giving them adequate support for innovations they choose to enact: This reflects the principals' respect for teachers as experts in the classroom, and it legitimizes teachers' professional status.

However, as administrators who fill bureaucratic positions, principals are compelled to assume responsibility over all matters in the school. Blase and Kirby (1992) found that the degree of autonomy granted to teachers by effective principals working in traditional schools ranged from substantial freedom to limited discretion over specific, defined issues. Similarly, they found that the degree of principal support for innovation ranged from a simple sanction to provision of extra materials and time.

What is significant is striking a balance between encouraging autonomy and innovation for teachers and the need for professional accountability. Mindful of this delicate balance, we suggest for consideration the following strategies for promoting healthy levels of autonomy and innovation in shared governance schools.

1. Use proactive strategies to promote autonomy and innovation.

Simply sanctioning autonomy and innovation is not enough. It is necessary to promote teacher autonomy and innovation through a variety of strategies: (a) provide formal decision-making structures, such as teams, committees, and special task forces; (b) provide professional development structures, such as workshops, conferences, and staff development sessions; (c) encourage informal interactions, including impromptu classroom visits and casual conversations about instructional concerns; and (d) suggest innovative ideas by providing copies of related articles to teachers.

2. Show support by involving yourself.

Shared governance principals reinforce their purposes by exhibiting trust, giving rewards, and showing sincere interest. But they also actively involve themselves in innovative activities. The following teacher comments describe this type of involvement:

> As an individual it's nice to have someone's presence to show support. Not only does the principal let us try things; she shows up to be a part of it. She comes to some of my after school activities, which shows my parents and me that she supports our activities.

> She listened intently when I was presenting something I'd like to try, offered helpful suggestions, and became a participant in the new program. I want to be constantly thinking of ways to improve.

3. Set high expectations; they need not be viewed as offensive.

In several instances, our teachers reported that although their principals clearly expected them to produce innovative decisions and actions, they did not consider such expectations offensive or intrusive. Principals described in our study and those described in a study of a recent school reform project (Goldman, Dunlap, & Conley, 1991) *assumed* that their teachers would be successful; they saw their own role as one of making professional collaboration possible, not one of creating obstacles and interfering. In addition, teacher trust and respect for principals, appreciation of principals' attempts to involve teachers in decision making, and the common goal of improving instruction—all outcomes of the empowerment process—seemed to prevent adverse reactions on the part of teachers to such expectations by principals.

4. Demonstrate dedication to improvement.

In our study, we found a strong connection between principals' enthusiasm and teacher empowerment, as reflected in the development of formal governance structures as well as in informal collegial relationships among teachers. One teacher remarked, "The principal's enthusiasm is contagious. She can make me feel that I am capable of accomplishing almost anything that I tackle." Such behavior, it appears, encourages teachers to do "great things" for the school and the students.

In fact, *shared governance principals rarely modeled or directly defined excellent teaching as a means of teacher improvement.* Rather, they facilitated teachers' abilities to improve programs, curriculum, teaching, and learning through their participation in school governance and innovative activities and especially in their enthusiasm for exciting new efforts.

References

Berliner, D. (1986). On the expert teacher: A conversation with David Berliner. *Educational Leadership, 44*(2), 4-9.

Blase, J., & Greenfield, W. (1981). An interactive/cyclical theory of teacher performance. *Administrator's Notebook, 29*(5), 1-4.

Blase, J., & Kirby, P. C. (1992). *Bringing out the best in teachers: What effective principals do.* Newbury Park, CA: Corwin.

Bredemeier, M. E. (1988). *Urban classroom portraits: Teachers who make a difference.* New York: P. Lang.

Goldman, P., Dunlap, D., & Conley, D. T. (1991, April). *Administrative facilitation and site-based school reform projects.* Paper presented at the annual meeting of the American Educational Research Association, Chicago.

Goodlad, J. I., Soder, J., & Sirotnik, K. A. (Eds.). (1990). *The moral dimensions of teaching.* San Francisco: Jossey-Bass.

Heck, R. H., Larsen, T. J., & Marcoulides, G. A. (1990). Instructional leadership and school achievement: Validation of a causal model. *Educational Administration Quarterly, 26*(2), 94-125.

Kidder, T. (1989). *Among schoolchildren.* Boston: Houghton Mifflin.

Lortie, D. C. (1975). *Schoolteacher: A sociological study.* Chicago: University of Chicago Press.

Mitchell, D. E., Ortiz, F. I., & Mitchell, T. K. (1987). *Work orientation and job performance: The cultural basis of teaching rewards and incentives.* Albany: State University of New York Press.

Rosenholtz, S. J. (1989). *Teachers' workplace: The social organization of schools.* New York: Longman.

Weick, K. E. (1976). Educational organizations as loosely coupled systems. *Administrative Science Quarterly, 21,* 1-19.

Wigginton, E. (1985). *Sometimes a shining moment: The Foxfire experience.* New York: Anchor/Doubleday.

6

Modeling Personal Dimensions

> Anyone who knows our principal can sense her love for what she does; she loves people and kids, especially. And her enthusiasm is contagious. She can make me feel that I'm capable of accomplishing almost anything that I tackle. I feel motivated and I keep working, planning, and trying to be better.
>
> —Middle School Teacher

Effective principals' first and foremost charge is *ensuring quality instruction* (Petrie, 1991), yet they also significantly *shape the climate* of the school (Wendel, Kilgore, & Spurzem, 1991). There is no doubt that providing a positive educational climate is a responsibility that successful principals enthusiastically embrace (Blase, 1987).

Bredeson (1989) interviewed 10 shared-decision principals to understand their view of teacher empowerment and its effects on their role as building administrators. He examined how principals' roles had been "reconceptualized and, informally renegotiated, and [were] continually being forged into new understandings of and working relationships with empowered teachers" (p. 9). His primary questions were the following:

Does teacher empowerment signal the end of the school principalship?
What changes and unique problems are there for principals working with empowered teachers?

What expectations do teachers and other stakeholders have of principals in teacher empowered schools? (pp. 15-17)

In one of the two districts he studied, Bredeson discovered that principals employed a limited problem-solving approach in their work with teachers; they typically identified problems for teachers and solicited teacher input. Policy and substantive instructional issues were not addressed in this district. In the second district, however, Bredeson found true empowerment, which was expressed as an *invitation to professionalism*. Here, principals' *modeling of professional behavior* in the day-to-day worklife patterns of the school fostered shared governance. Bredeson concluded that

> rethinking and redefining the principal's leadership role in schools in which teachers exercise significant professional autonomy and share in governance and decision making are critical to the nurture of empowerment and to the attainment of desired educational outcomes. (p. 14)

Furthermore, Bredeson identified nine important themes regarding the role of the principal in fostering teacher empowerment:

- Use the language of shared governance and empowerment
- Establish readiness for professional growth and empowerment
- Secure the superintendent's leadership in empowerment
- Use time as a key resource for empowerment
- Engage in boundary spanning across publics and institutions
- Enhance teachers' and principals' professional image
- Listen and attend to teachers' concerns
- Encourage sharing of professional thinking
- Deal with power through empowerment

Bredeson also found that principals believed that teachers expected them to be reassuring, trusting, and patient and wanted them to "stay out of their way," "trust them," "allow mistakes," and "let things happen" (p. 17).

Many of Bredeson's general themes are embodied in this book, and all relate to the behavior of principals we describe. More specifically, however, we found that certain personal characteristics of successful shared governance principals contributed to teachers' sense of empowerment: optimism, caring, honesty, friendliness, and enthusiasm. These characteristics may not have been intentionally employed as strategies by principals to enhance teacher empowerment; however, they were viewed as having "strategic significance" (i.e., impact) for teachers (Blase, 1991). They form the basis for a model shared governance principal.

A Model Shared Governance Principal

Advocates of shared governance stress that making use of teachers' expertise and experience will result in better schooling for our youth. However, the personal characteristics of principals who tap this resource to create a rich and vital "community of leaders" (Barth, 1988) have been largely ignored. As noted, our data suggest that five primary personal characteristics of successful shared governance principals were especially powerful in facilitating teacher empowerment: optimism, caring, honesty, friendliness, and enthusiasm.

Optimism

Optimistic principals tended to emphasize the *positive* aspects of situations. They believed that teachers would "responsibly" participate in shared governance as a valid approach to organizational and educational improvement. Optimistic principals also expected teachers to *aggressively* pursue their ongoing commitment to improve teaching and learning. In particular (as covered in Chapter 5), they consistently helped teachers prepare for the occasional but inevitable "failure" that accompanies innovation and experimentation in shared governance schools. One teacher attested:

> [Our principal] provides an atmosphere of positive *feelings that anything can be accomplished.* This empowers me to try new and exciting teaching strategies. If these strategies are not

successful, I am confident that my principal will thank me for trying and *reinforce the positive aspects* of the experience. (emphasis added)

Caring

Caring describes the principal's *sincere interest* in teachers' professional and personal problems. It reflects an understanding of the holistic interrelatedness of teachers' work and personal life. Two teachers' comments illustrate this characteristic (all emphases added throughout):

> She is frequently in the classroom to "walk through," not necessarily in a judgmental role but in a *curious* capacity—as if your teaching techniques and your daily activities are *of extreme interest to her.*

> Our principal communicates with us as a staff and as individuals. This *"personal touch"* helps build my sense of empowerment because it establishes a foundation for mutual respect. It helps make you feel comfortable about discussing classroom problems because you feel that she values your feelings and opinions. Her sensitivity helps you feel empowered *because you can tell she has great desire to help teachers succeed.*

Honesty

Principals' openness, their straightforwardness in professional interactions with teachers, was quite important in empowering teachers. Honesty was considered central to productive communication between teachers and principals. Teachers reported that without honesty—particularly when principals were inaccessible, failed to support teachers, and exhibited favoritism—discussion, debate, and decision making were distorted and even undermined. *Interestingly, our findings suggest that conflict increases (becomes more overt) between principals and teachers as authentic participation in schoolwide governance structures expands.* Under these circumstances, principals' honesty seemed to increase the probability of a productive approach to conflict. As one teacher put it,

> The principal doesn't lie to me or try to smooth things over just to "shut me up." He *engages in open, honest dialogue about differences.* (emphasis added)

Friendliness

Friendliness was defined as a warm, easy, accepting interpersonal orientation that provokes feelings of satisfaction and confidence in teachers. Teachers reported working harder because of the friendliness and positive regard exhibited by principals. Other impacts of principal friendliness were reflected in improved teacher self-esteem and teacher ownership of schoolwide concerns. The following teachers' comments describe friendliness:

> He is *friendly*—has lunch with me, casual conversations before school, visits in the teachers' lounge. I am not fearful of him in any way. I would feel at ease in discussing any matter of concern to me or making any suggestions about our school to him.

> She *makes me feel comfortable* socially. Therefore, I feel I can communicate easily with her. This rapport instills a confidence in me—from her ability to handle making decisions and leading groups.

> She has a cheery attitude, almost always smiling, and always *considerate and pleasant.* This gives me encouragement to ask for help with my problems. She is not forbidding.

An important by-product of principal friendliness was the reduction of status differences between principals and teachers. According to our data, de-emphasizing hierarchical positions "freed" teachers to participate confidently in schoolwide decision making.

Enthusiasm

Shared governance principals exhibited enthusiasm—high motivation and personal dedication to improve teaching and learning and to enhance teacher empowerment. Enthusiasm was demonstrated primarily through (a) the active development of formal, shared governance structures (see Chapter 3 for a detailed discussion) and (b) the development and maintenance of supportive, collegial relationships with teachers. Rarely were principals seen as modeling or directly defining excellent teaching; instead, they *indirectly* supported teachers' efforts to improve instruction through their participation in school governance and influence on work in classrooms. The comments of two teachers exemplify the impact of principals' enthusiasm on teachers:

> Her *enthusiasm is contagious.* She can make me feel that I am capable of accomplishing almost anything that I tackle.

> Her attitude was always *positive and encouraging* to the point that I always wanted to go beyond for the school and the student.

Teacher Responses

Principals' optimism, caring, honesty, friendliness, and enthusiasm enhanced teachers' work in both the classroom and the school at large. As a consequence, teachers' self-esteem, confidence, and satisfaction were enhanced. These personal behaviors have significant effects on teacher empowerment and are discussed below.

Self-Esteem

The most frequently discussed result of principals' positive personal characteristics was increased self-esteem. This refers to the teacher's sense of "importance" and "significance"; teachers used terms such as "valued," "important," and "worthy" to denote self-esteem.

Self-esteem was identified with increased teacher involvement in the classroom and in schoolwide governance. Teachers wrote, "I matter," "I count," and "I feel important in my job. This is more than just coming and learning. I am important." The personal characteristic of *caring*, in particular, was linked to positive teacher self-esteem. Two teachers commented,

> She really cares about people and loves her job. I *feel like an important member* of the staff.

> She genuinely seems to have a concern for me on a personal level. She asks about my family and is concerned about my well-being. *I feel like I matter* to her and the school.

Confidence

Greater teacher confidence—feelings of "competence" and "independence"—was associated with several personal characteristics of principals. Teacher confidence developed within the context of classroom decision making, particularly decision making related to innovative instruction. Principal caring had the most powerful impact on teacher confidence, as one teacher said,

> My principal seems to be interested in me as a person as well as an employee. I don't feel threatened to go to my principal with problems. This made me *confident* to perform my duties. (emphasis added)

Satisfaction

Principals' caring, optimism, and friendliness brought feelings of satisfaction to teachers. Terms such as "satisfied," "happy," "good," "thankful," "positive," "enjoyable," and "pleased" were used to denote feelings of satisfaction. Typically, satisfaction was discussed in terms of successes in the classroom. In one teacher's opinion,

> My thoughts are positive towards work because my principal instills a caring, positive attitude by setting an example.

I *enjoy* my work, instead of feeling like I'm doing time. (emphasis added)

A Pitfall to Creating a Climate for Success: Letting Go and Role Strain

Successful shared governance principals seem to understand the potential of a school. They affect the culture or character of the organization, and they reflect upon and use problem-solving processes to examine alternative actions. Furthermore, such leaders help to transform the school by actively building group cooperation and spirit (Pajak, 1993). Yet as they do this these principals sometimes have concerns about "letting go," about giving people a chance to solve their own problems. Naturally, principals can be expected to experience a sense of loss as they give power to others.

Bredeson (1993) has shown that difficulties in letting go can produce *role strain* in principals. In a study of 20 principals involved in restructuring efforts, he discovered that principals' expectations, norms, and values differed between old and new role sets. When principals' role expectations changed they experienced *role strain*, which was manifested as anxiety and general distress. Specifically, the varying states and levels of anxiety were evident in *feelings of having lost control, fear of failure, self-doubts about personal competence, impatience and frustration, concerns about loss of professional identity,* and *feelings of uncertainty.*

Bredeson reported, "The notion of letting go of one set of professional functions and identities while learning others was described as risky, wearisome, and frustrating" (p. 46). Thus the principal with the best intentions of being optimistic, caring, honest, friendly, and enthusiastic—that is, generally supportive—may find it difficult to do so while letting go of an older role.

Bergman (1992) investigated a small elementary school in New Jersey involved in a site-based management initiative generally consistent with shared governance guidelines. Although the school principal had reservations and anxieties about "letting go," faculty and staff members *gradually* built a culture of supportive interpersonal relationships and collaboration in the following ways:

1. Creating a leadership council composed of teachers, parents, staff members, board members, and a central office administrator

2. Developing a school philosophy by working together cooperatively and, among other things, practicing good communication skills, such as active listening and paraphrasing

3. Gathering feedback from community members, parents, and teachers

4. Allowing group members to clarify perceptions about work and relationships as well as to understand each other's styles and promoting open communication and trust by allowing members to think with new perspectives and take time for reflection

In sum, restructuring for shared governance carries with it many potential psychological, social, and micropolitical consequences. Attention to transition factors that affect principals' as well as teachers' professional lives is critical to the success of shared governance. A willingness to address these issues must go hand in hand with a collaborative approach to building a positive and productive work atmosphere.

Tips From Teachers

According to the teachers in our study, successful shared governance principals are models of optimism, caring, honesty, friendliness, and enthusiasm. The significant effects of such behaviors can be enhanced by the following actions, all of which are tips from teachers:

1. Establish your role early.

Discuss your role with faculty and staff members early in the shared governance process. The primary change in your role may well be that you will be working more indirectly (i.e., "behind the scenes" instead of "in the lead") as you share decision making with teachers. Once decisions have been made, more individuals and groups will be ready to work on problems. This frees you, in a sense, to be a *facilitator of improvement efforts. The result can be improved student achievement and a sense of joy that comes from success and accomplishment on the part of teachers.*

2. Be positive, supportive, and warm.

Besides the personal characteristics of optimism, caring, honesty, friendliness, and enthusiasm, several other ingredients are necessary in successful shared governance enterprises. These include the principal's unconditional positive regard, interpersonal warmth, and broad support and encouragement of teachers. As principals work to create an excellent learning environment for students they sometimes overlook the importance of providing a supportive, caring work environment for teachers (Sarason, 1990). However, effective principals can create school environments in which students as well as teachers can thrive (Blase, 1987; Licata, Teddlie, & Greenfield, 1990).

3. Communicate a feeling of freedom.

The school culture must communicate a feeling of freedom—to risk, to experiment, to share ideas and feelings. Because principals have a great deal of influence on a school's culture (Mitchell & Tucker, 1992) they should encourage a climate of sound instructional improvement, balanced and integrated with deep concern for all involved in collegial efforts to enhance instruction and student growth. This is the way professionalism flourishes.

4. Find time to relax.

Initiating shared governance processes in a school is time-consuming and challenging. Leaders who help others initiate this approach must also keep themselves strong and energized. Accept that uncertainty is a natural part of the process in its early stages, and take care of yourself as well as others.

References

Barth, R. S. (1988). Principals, teachers, and school leadership. *Phi Delta Kappan, 69*(9), 639-642.

Bergman, A. B. (1992). Lessons for principals from site-based management. *Educational Leadership, 50*(1), 48-51.

Blase, J. (1987). Dimensions of effective school leadership: The teachers' perspective. *American Educational Research Journal, 24*(4), 589-610.

Blase, J. (1991). Analysis and discussion: Some concluding remarks. In J. Blase (Ed.), *The politics of life in schools: Power, conflict, and cooperation* (pp. 237-255). Newbury Park, CA: Sage.

Bredeson, P. V. (1989). Redefining leadership and the roles of school principals: Responses to changes in the professional worklife of teachers. *The High School Journal, 73*(1), 9-20.

Bredeson, P. V. (1993). Letting go of outlived professional identities: A study of role transition and role strain for principals in restructured schools. *Educational Administration Quarterly, 29*(1), 34-68.

Licata, J. W., Teddlie, C. B., & Greenfield, W. D. (1990). Principal vision, teacher sense of autonomy, and environmental robustness. *Journal of Educational Research, 84*(2), 93-99.

Mitchell, D., & Tucker, S. (1992). Leadership as a way of thinking. *Educational Leadership, 49*(5), 30-35.

Pajak, E. (1993). Change and continuity in supervision and leadership. In G. Cawelty (Ed.), *Challenges and achievements of American education* (pp. 158-186). Alexandria, VA: Association for Supervision and Curriculum Development.

Petrie, T. A. (1991). A return to the principalship: Professor relates plans for change. *NASSP Bulletin, 75*(539), 44-51.

Sarason, S. B. (1990). *The predictable failure of educational reform: Can we change courses before it's too late?* San Francisco: Jossey-Bass.

Wendel, F. C., Kilgore, A. M., & Spurzem, C. W. (1991). Are administrators' personalities related to their job skills? *NASSP Bulletin, 75*(539), 14-20.

7

About Risk and Threat

One characteristic that my principal displays is her lack of fear for experimentation; this sense of experimentation allows teachers the luxury of exploring ideas. If a teacher or group of teachers propose an idea to her which is feasible, she is most willing to place the idea into effect on a trial basis and implement the idea later if it has proven to be successful. Even though our ideas are often successful, there are some which are not as successful; these are the ideas that are molded, altered, and revised until there is a clear, workable solution.

—Elementary School Teacher

In a powerful and popular book that draws a rich portrait of "the good high school," Sara Lightfoot (1983) aptly captured the essence of the creativity, responsiveness, and willpower of teachers. She further described teachers' sincere caring and commitment to students and concluded that those who invest heavily in the school organization tend to be *risk takers.*

The particular type of commitment that Lightfoot describes seems to be critical to the effective functioning of individuals, groups, and the school in general (Reyes, 1990). It is represented as deep dedication to the school, an activity, or a task, and it involves a commitment to improvement. *Without risk, there can be no improvement*, and "good" teachers know this intuitively. Successful shared governance principals *support the need for experimentation and risk taking,* whereas ineffective principals are inclined to thwart teachers' efforts to try new and different things (Blase, 1987).

Negative Behaviors of Ineffective Principals

Reflective, improvement-oriented practice is a high-risk process that goes "against the grain" of most organizations (Argyris, 1990). Weakness or incompetence may be revealed in conversations about problems. Without high trust and openness people do not feel safe and secure; hence they take no risks. The behavior of principals in such situations is remarkably similar. When teachers described former principals in our study, they offered the following reports (all emphases added throughout):

> My previous principal would *undermine my decisions* regarding student trips, et cetera.

> I feel that in other schools where I have taught the principal *didn't give you much freedom* on your class rules or discipline procedures.

> She was always *scrutinizing* plan books or snooping. She required plans to be turned in early. She did a random check and *made criticisms.*

> When a teacher feels *unappreciated* and is *dealt with coldly*— "by the book"—it makes you feel withdrawn. Our principal expected lots of extra time and work but never came by to express appreciation or give something (like leaving early or arriving late) as a reward.

An examination of the *positive* behaviors of shared governance principals yields additional insights into what behaviors teachers feel are constraining. The following statements about these principals contain clues to the contrasting offensive and oppressive behaviors of former principals who maintained control and squelched reflection and creativity:

I do not feel *threatened* by my principal's presence. I love to have him visit my classroom and see my ideas at work.

I know he's not going to *scream and yell* at me.

I don't *feel ashamed* if I don't follow my lesson plans to the letter. He trusts me to make adjustments as needed.

I have never heard him *speak poorly* of another teacher or peer.

He does not *monitor* classroom activities constantly or demand detailed and extensive *plans and reports* from the faculty.

I am not *fearful* of him in any way. I would feel at ease in discussing any matter of concern to me or making any suggestion about our school to him.

The principal doesn't *tell me specifically how to do my job* because I think he feels I know how to perform the necessary duties.

I don't *feel threatened* to go to my principal with problems. I don't feel my principal will *criticize* me for my mistakes.

The principal does not convey the idea that *he knows everything,* with teachers as peons.

My principal's nonthreatening behavior contributes to my sense of empowerment. He does not try to *intimidate* me when he answers a question, but exhibits respect and acceptance of me as an individual.

He doesn't ever *say "That won't work,"* and that's it for us. We have input.

He doesn't *lie to me* or try to smooth things over just to shut me up. He engages in open, honest dialogue about the difference.

The types of negative and positive behaviors described above are consistent with a theoretical framework developed by Argyris and Schön (1974). These researchers described two contrasting theories of interpersonal behavior in organizational settings: Model I and Model II. Model I leadership behaviors are described as restrictive, judgmental, and controlling; they generate defensive relationships and mistrust. Examples of Model I behaviors are withholding critical information and avoiding discussing problems or concerns to keep things under control and protect oneself. Such behaviors do not support the development of a community committed to professional growth and development (Argyris, 1990; Senge, 1990).

Positive Behaviors
of Successful Shared Governance Principals

By contrast, Model II behaviors, such as openly sharing information, tend to improve the quality of interpersonal relations, stimulate professional growth, and enhance a school's effectiveness. Model II behaviors encourage trust, collaboration, and effective problem solving (Blase & Kirby, 1992; Jentz, 1982; Osterman, 1991; Parkay & Hall, 1992). Examples of these types of behavior can be seen in the work of effective principals who visit classrooms and provide feedback to teachers after their visits. Blase and Kirby (1992) noted that teachers found this practice acceptable because it was accompanied by genuine interest and support; it was not viewed as obtrusive or punitive. Teachers associated such behavior with "opportunities for improvement" (p. 108).

In other words, positive or negative information about performance needs to be willingly received (as well as risk- and threat-free) so that it can give professionals the knowledge necessary to create change for improvement. Schön (1983) stated,

> When a practitioner becomes a researcher into his [or her] own practice, he [or she] engages in a continuing process of self-education. . . . the recognition of error, with its resulting uncertainty, can become a source of discovery rather than an occasion for self defense. (p. 299)

Respondents in our study often discussed the critical link between the actions of shared governance principals and the development of risk-free environments and improved teaching in their schools:

> She *values my opinions and ideas* and allows me to share them with her without fear of reprisal or criticism even when our opinions differ.

> I am more willing to risk something that may or may not work! I try new things and *don't worry* that if something doesn't work as well as I hoped, it will be met with negativity.

> I *feel free to try new things* and go to [the principal] with problems. If he were a person here to criticize my wrongs, I would be too intimidated to try new things or go to him. When I do need to see him with a problem or question, I do not feel any less a professional because I have consulted him.

> Our principal *gave permission* to try new things. Risk taking was *encouraged* with the understanding that the responsibility came with it. This is necessary in order to produce good teaching school wide. Teachers who don't feel this will shut down and go through "the drill," feeling that the work is out of their control, and that if their job is to get kids through the system the learning goes by the wayside.

Moving Toward
Shared Governance Assumptions

In describing a school staff involved in democratic governance and whose behavior approximated Model II assumptions, Osterman and Kottkamp (1993) spoke of the "uncharted waters and the evolving mystery" (p. 142) associated with the process of group development. They described the eventual emergence of a level of functioning characterized by authentic engagement in and strong commitment to the work of the school, a willingness to explore and take risks, playfulness and humor, an openness to new information coupled with incisive intellectual probing, and interpersonal trust and an openness to exploring emotions as well as thoughts (p. 147).

Osterman and Kottkamp concluded that the factors noted above were strongly related to risk taking and always helped the group arrive at meaningful conclusions. These factors were mentioned consistently throughout our data as well and were described in terms of their positive effects on group functioning in the schools studied.

Responding to
Basic Motivational Needs: Reflective Practice

Theorists have described several basic human motivational needs, including competence (experiencing oneself as capable of producing worthy and useful outcomes), autonomy (having control over one's activities as well as consistency among one's actions, goals, and values), and relatedness (having social connections that confirm one's worthiness for love and respect) (Connell & Wellborn, 1989). By creating an environment open to taking risks and free of threat, a shared governance principal paves the way for teacher empowerment. Teachers feel a sense of professionalism and are proud to be teachers.

In a study of reflective practices, Berkey et al. (1990) quote one teacher's remarks:

> I gained so much confidence in myself, and I learned to
> respect myself as a professional and to trust my knowledge,
> that I have the courage to take risks, to try new things, and
> to be vulnerable. I no longer need to strive to be someone
> else's ideal model of a teacher, but I can strive to be the best
> teacher I can be. (p. 220)

Berkey et al. indicated that significant changes were also evident in students. Recognizing that they were in a nonthreatening learning environment, *students* were more comfortable with taking risks and meeting challenges. The practice of lowering threat and anxiety also seemed to lend itself to greater *teacher reflection*. And reflective practice contributes to each of the basic motivational needs of competence, autonomy, and relatedness. Osterman and Kottkamp (1993) offer this description of reflective practice:

> [It] provides the information needed for people to effect posi-
> tive changes in performance; it respects the right of individu-
> als to exercise self-direction and, in fact, enhances their ability
> to exercise control over their own actions. Finally, it engages
> people in a collaborative process of professional development
> that responds to their needs for relatedness and increases
> their sense of efficacy. (p. 185)

In related work on effects of leadership behaviors, Blase (1993) found that only three strategies used by effective principals in tradi-tional schools—suggestion, encouraging input, and empowering teachers to make decisions—enhanced teacher reflection.

Navigating in Uncharted Waters

The uncharted waters of school improvement may seem to be a very intimidating place. Consider the following suggestions as you strive to support risk and lower threat:

1. Trust that teachers are learners who will take responsibility.

In Chapter 2, trust was discussed as the foundation upon which all meaningful school work is built. Most teachers want to improve, and they desperately want to be authentically involved in the work of making the school a better place for all to live and learn. Teachers will take great responsibility for such improvement just as they shoulder tremendous responsibility for many young lives every day. Remember that *expecting* the best usually brings out the best.

2. Become more of a facilitator.

Principals can exhibit less "direct" leadership behavior as time passes. As people become more comfortable with reflection and risk taking, a principal can begin to fulfill the role of a *facilitator* rather than a boss. This can be done by supporting teachers with encouragement, resources, thoughtful discussion, and many opportunities for collaborative problem solving.

3. Model behaviors that spring from shared governance assumptions.

Successful shared governance principals freely share information and welcome efforts to improve. They do not narrow options, limit opportunities, or avoid issues. In the interest of improvement, they become open, even welcoming, to sharing and examining important data, analyzing problems, and planning for improvement.

4. Consider that this can be a quiet change.

Sometimes, the most tremendous changes come from merely enhancing people's opportunities to reflect on practice and discuss possibilities. The great potential inherent in any group of professional teachers can be tapped quietly in a dedicated effort to look carefully at what is being done and how it might be made better.

5. Personify hope.

Be prepared to risk changing and always indicate your immutable belief that teachers:

- have the requisite *knowledge* to effect positive change
- have the *ability* to make significant and important educational and organizational changes
- are *committed* to providing the best possible education for their students
- are *eager to participate* in collegial decision making for school-wide issues
- deserve protected *time* for reflection and collaboration

6. Cultivate grace.

People of grace recognize (and stand in awe of) significant elements inherent in the smallest of things. The ability to see wondrous possibilities and seize on serendipitous opportunities is a talent of those with grace. Continuously look about you for such potentialities and sensitize others to them; fine solutions to our problems may lie in tiny moments or in the heart of the quietest person among us.

7. Tolerate ambiguity.

A professional is trained to *cope with uncertainty*. Some leaders, however, mistakenly worry that involving teachers in decision making will undermine their ability to control. Successful shared governance principals come to grips with the real-life uncertainties that exist in schools as well as the professional teacher's ability to make wise decisions, given a myriad of unstable contextual factors.

References

Argyris, C. (1990). *Overcoming organizational defenses: Facilitating organizational learning*. Needham, MA: Allyn & Bacon.

Argyris, C., & Schön, D. A. (1974). *Theory in practice: Increasing professional effectiveness*. San Francisco: Jossey-Bass.

Berkey, R., Campbell, D., Curtis, T., Kirschner, B. W., Minnick, F., & Zietlow, K. (1990). Collaborating for reflective practice: Voices of teachers, administrators, and researchers. *Education & Urban Society, 22*(2), 204-232.

Blase, J. (1987). Dimensions of ineffective school leadership: The teachers' perspective. *Journal of Educational Administration, 25*(2), 193-213.

Blase, J. (1993). The micropolitics of effective school-based leadership: Teachers' perspectives. *Educational Administration Quarterly, 29*(2), 142-163.

Blase, J., & Kirby, P. C. (1992). *Bringing out the best in teachers: What effective principals do*. Newbury Park, CA: Corwin.

Connell, J. P., & Wellborn, J. G. (1989, April). *Competence, autonomy, and relatedness*. Paper presented at the annual meeting of the American Educational Research Association, San Francisco.

Jentz, B. (1982). *The hiring, start-up, and supervision of administrators.* New York: McGraw-Hill.

Lightfoot, S. L. (1983). *The good high school: Portraits of character and culture.* New York: Basic Books.

Osterman, K. F. (1991). Case records: A means to enhance the knowledge base in educational administration. In F. C. Wendel (Ed.), *Enhancing the knowledge base in educational administration* (pp. 35-47). University Park, PA: University Council for Educational Administration.

Osterman, K. F., & Kottkamp, R. B. (1993). *Reflective practice for educators: Improving schooling through professional development.* Newbury Park, CA: Corwin.

Parkay, F. W., & Hall, G. E. (1992). *Becoming a principal: The challenges of beginning leadership.* Needham Heights, MA: Allyn & Bacon.

Reyes, P. (1990). Linking commitment, performance, and productivity. In P. Reyes (Ed.), *Teachers and their workplace: Commitment, performance, and productivity* (pp. 299-311). Newbury Park, CA: Sage.

Schön, D. A. (1983). *The reflective practitioner: How professionals think in action.* New York: Basic Books.

Senge, P. M. (1990). The leader's new work: Building learning organizations. *Sloan Management Review, 32*(1), 7-23.

8

Valuing and Rewarding Good Work

Our principal is very thoughtful and appreciative. She frequently writes notes of appreciation for specific things as well as simply to let me know that she is glad to be working with me. It is humbling, motivating, and encouraging to know that your efforts have been noticed. I feel appreciated and thankful to be working with such a caring, considerate person. She is so excited and positive! I work harder and I want to find new, better ways to do what I do.

—Middle School Teacher

Ernest Boyer (1983) has recommended that the working conditions of teachers should be improved by reducing class load, increasing preparation time, decreasing isolation, improving intellectual opportunities, decreasing routine tasks, improving salaries, creating a career path, and *recognizing and rewarding teachers' good work and ideas.* In *900 Shows a Year: A Look at Teaching From a Teacher's Side of the Desk*, Palonsky (1986) recommended that teachers should be given more voice in the school decision-making structure and that *good teachers should be given more recognition and encouragement.*

With many teachers leaving the profession (or indicating an interest in doing so) every year (Grant, 1988) and with the majority of teaching vacancies filled by recent graduates (Darling-Hammond, 1988), the retention of effective teachers has become problematic. Our study produced unequivocal evidence that a principal's *use of rewards* has the primary effects of facilitating teacher empowerment in shared governance schools; creating teacher satisfaction, a motivation to work harder, a sense of efficacy, and self-esteem; and counteracting teacher dissatisfaction.

In this chapter we examine the power of praising, valuing, and respecting teachers; the various forms shared governance principals use to reward teachers symbolically; and the specific effects of such rewards on teacher empowerment. We posit that the retention of effective teachers may be significantly enhanced by the proper and judicious use of rewards.

The Relationship Between Reward and Empowerment

To some it may seem that principals' use of reward and their empowerment of teachers are contradictory or mutually exclusive. After all, in shared governance schools, empowered teachers make decisions and act according to their professional judgments on what is in the best interests of the students. Their behavior is not supposed to be *contingent* upon a leader (principal) who allocates rewards for what they do. In contrast to being "objects," as they were often viewed in their role as followers (Smyth, 1989, 1990), empowered teachers are supposed to be transformed into active, self-determining professionals. Some research has even indicated a negative correlation between the manipulation of rewards by principals and teacher morale, autonomy, classroom resources, schoolwide expression, work involvement, and teacher-administrator relationships (e.g., Blase, 1990; Stimson & Appelbaum, 1988).

The Rewards of a Career in Teaching

The rewards of an individual's job can be classified as *extrinsic* (salary, working hours, status, and power) or *intrinsic* (psychic or subjective rewards). Teaching is limited in extrinsic rewards, but the intrinsic rewards include knowing that students are learning, emotional attachment to students, interaction with colleagues, satisfaction in performing a valuable service, enjoyment of teaching activities, and enjoyment of learning from teaching (Feiman-Nemser & Floden, 1986; Lortie, 1975).

Our findings demonstrate that successful shared governance principals make extrinsic and intrinsic rewards possible for teachers. Participative decision making increases teacher status and power, and collegial problem solving focused on instructional improvement leads to myriad psychic rewards for teachers. Furthermore, the simple but *sincere* act of "praising" teachers appears to be a primary, effective, and valued form of reward for teaching.

Rewarding by Praising and Valuing/Respecting Teachers

Shared governance principals take every opportunity available to *praise* or demonstrate value and respect for teachers for their professional performance. The variety of opportunities and methods of praising teachers seems to be unlimited. The most direct methods include complimenting teachers at faculty meetings, in formal and informal conferences, in faculty lounges and at school functions, and in public announcements over the intercom: "Our principal takes time to announce the successes and honors of her faculty on the morning announcements." Teachers frequently remarked that praise was expressed by principals *regularly*, usually through notes of appreciation and verbal "pats on the back." Praise was also conveyed in the form of complimentary remarks to third parties.

Shared governance principals used praise to do the following:

- Recognize special successes ("She has recommended me for such awards as the Presidential Teacher of Excellence.")
- Acknowledge work above and beyond one's duty ("She makes every effort to assist and acknowledge involvement in the local system.")

- Recognize the unique contributions and individuality of teachers ("She recognizes the different contributions that different people can make.")
- Recognize the day-to-day challenges and difficulties that teachers encounter in their work ("The principal makes opportunities to tell us that she is aware of the difficulties we deal with and that she appreciates the work that we do.")

As evidenced by the remarks of several teachers, shared governance principals express praise in many ways both verbally and nonverbally but nevertheless effectively. The last quote above suggests the impact of principals' praise was enhanced substantially by the recognition of teaching challenges. Praise was also given by some principals to "simply let you know that she is glad to be working with you."

The comments of teachers in our study often paralleled those of teachers in Blase and Kirby's (1992) effective principal study. For example, *although praise was seen as a strategy used by principals to influence teachers in predetermined directions, the fact that it was given "sincerely" by effective traditional principals made it significant.* Frank, unabashed admiration for teachers' expertise and skills is never a controlling, bureaucratic, or political ploy! However, it is important to note that shared governance principals use rewards for the purpose of empowering teachers, not controlling them.

Effects on Teachers

Teachers who participated in our study reported that praise and other symbolic rewards (valuing, respecting) influenced them primarily when these rewards were related to their *professional* performance. One effect of praise was an increase in teachers' inclination to work harder (all emphases added throughout):

My ideas are valued; therefore I am more willing to spend many hours beyond what is required working on school-related business.

> It is very nice to hear a *thank you* for the work that I do! I work harder.

A second effect of praise was teachers' increased sense of efficacy:

> My principal communicates with me. Recently, I received a note that thanked me for sharing and commented on my ideas. When I am *recognized* I feel that I am contributing as a facilitator of change.

Praise also yielded greater teacher self-esteem:

> Our observations and suggestions are respected. This makes us feel that we have opportunities to make changes and that new ideas will not be heard then forgotten. I think of myself as *important and capable*.

> I feel that my judgments are primary, not subject to her administrative approval. I feel confident in my judgments. I think of myself as a competent decision maker.

Finally, principals' demonstrations of valuing and respecting teachers (and their attitude of being *colearners*) increased motivation:

> The principal is visible . . . frequently in the classrooms. To have your administrator engaged in your day-to-day work provides a bridge between administration and faculty. I am more often involved in "on-task" behaviors during the day than in other school employment positions I've occupied.

> The principal is aware of the hours I keep and of the constant communication I attempt with my learners and their families. This helps me feel like her colleague, her peer. I'm not just some hired help that comes and goes. *Her awareness is filled with gratitude*—not a feeling of being checked upon. I work more willingly and display a more positive attitude.

Because symbolic rewards frequently took the form of giving teachers praise and respect (including demonstrating an interest in and appreciation for teachers' work and respecting their thinking), shared governance principals were able to enhance teachers' sense of empowerment. As a result, teachers reported devoting more time and energy to both classroom and schoolwide matters, demanding higher-quality work from themselves, and experiencing a greater sense of personal importance and job enjoyment.

Teacher Dissatisfaction: Caveats About Rewards

A study by May (1990) explored the reasons why one very talented teacher left the profession. These reasons were (a) administrative decisions and parental pressure that undermined her efforts to provide a quality education to students, (b) frustration with the ineffectiveness of committees despite the tremendous amount of work required, (c) feelings of humiliation and being undervalued by administrators, and (d) the feeling of being "used" by administrators (i.e., *her reward for good work was more work*).

With regard to the last reason, the teacher experienced severe emotional strain from being *appreciated* one minute and *overworked* the next. This same problem was described in our data. We learned that the strategy of extending symbolic *rewards* can be a powerful tool in implementing shared governance structures and motivating teachers *as long as it is not accompanied by increased and unreasonable professional expectations*.

An additional caveat about rewards deserves mention. Blase and Kirby (1992) indicated that effective principals *do not use group praise* to compensate for a lack of individual praise and consistently influence teachers through the use of praise *related to their professional accomplishments* (in contrast to personal compliments or praise for accomplishments outside school). These ideas should be viewed as caveats in using rewards to enhance teacher empowerment. Otherwise, instead of increasing job satisfaction, rewarding teachers may create emotional ambivalence or confusion and uncertainty.

Guidelines for Effective
Use of Symbolic Rewards

Praising, valuing, and respecting teachers are forms of reward that have powerful effects. The following guidelines, derived from teachers' comments, will enable you to enhance your efforts to support teachers through reward.

1. Keep abreast of teacher activities.

Shared governance principals devote ample time to becoming informed about teacher activities and contributions. Because they are aware of teachers' myriad efforts and achievements these principals frequently seize opportunities to compliment, reward, and even boast about teachers.

2. Limit assignments for already overloaded teachers.

As noted earlier, being given additional assignments after receiving praise for one's work can be offensive to and stressful for teachers. Reward good work with some form of relief from routine duties, if possible. This motivates teachers and frees them to concentrate on areas in which they can have the most positive impact. Also, strive to award more *authority* to teachers, not more work.

3. Relate rewards to professional achievements.

Teachers who demonstrate initiative, creativity, genuine involvement, and leadership are contributing to the goals we all hold for the school and for students. Rewarding professionalism in teaching evokes a strong response on the part of teachers; they become more satisfied and motivated and feel greater self-esteem.

4. Recognize teachers' work frequently.

Teachers reported that shared governance principals communicate praise regularly through the public address system, at meetings, or on informal walk-throughs and classroom visits. Consistently making an effort to recognize teachers' hard work and successes is a hallmark of leadership.

5. Use many avenues of reward.

Although opportunities for the use of tangible rewards may be limited for teachers, principals can diversify and maximize the reward opportunities available to them. Authority in making decisions, recognition and respect, and praise for the valuable work of teachers all constitute extrinsic rewards for teachers. More potent, however, are the intrinsic rewards that teachers derive from their work; principals can provide opportunities for interaction with colleagues and minimize barriers to teachers' enjoyment of teaching.

References

Blase, J. (1990). Some negative effects of principals' control-oriented and protective political behavior: The teachers' perspective. *American Educational Research Journal, 27*(4), 727-753.

Blase, J., & Kirby, P. C. (1992). *Bringing out the best in teachers: What effective principals do.* Newbury Park, CA: Corwin.

Boyer, E. L. (1983). *High school: A report on secondary education in America.* New York: Harper & Row.

Darling-Hammond, L. (1988). The futures of teaching. *Educational Leadership, 46*(3), 4-10.

Feiman-Nemser, S., & Floden, R. E. (1986). The cultures of teaching. In M. C. Wittrock (Ed.), *Handbook of research on teaching* (3rd ed., pp. 505-526). New York: Macmillan.

Grant, G. (1988). *The world we created at Hamilton High.* Cambridge, MA: Harvard University Press.

Lortie, D. C. (1975). *School teacher: A sociological study.* Chicago: University of Chicago Press.

May, J. (1990, April). *Education failed me: Career history of a teacher who left the profession.* Paper presented at the annual meeting of the American Educational Research Association, Boston.

Palonsky, S. B. (1986). *900 shows a year: A look at teaching from a teacher's side of the desk.* New York: Random House.

Smyth, J. (Ed.). (1989). *Critical perspectives on educational leadership.* London: Falmer Press.

Smyth, J. (1990, April). *A pedagogical and educative view of leadership.* Paper presented at the annual meeting of the American Educational Research Association, Boston.

Stimson, T. D., & Appelbaum, R. P. (1988). Empowering teachers: Do principals have the power? *Phi Delta Kappan, 70,* 313-316.

9

Helping Solve Problems

Our principal is very quick to put into action and to recognize any good plans for solving a problem. He will set up a task force to review and come up with solutions, set deadlines, and quickly bring the plan to the entire faculty for implementation. He has met with parents, reviewed options, and implemented innovative plans. I feel confident that my problems and concerns will be taken seriously and dealt with, and that I have a chance to offer suggestions; if they are valuable they will be put into action. I am more likely to share my ideas and solutions and to concentrate on problem-solving myself.

—Middle School Teacher

As noted earlier, Melenyzer (1990) has described three general perspectives on teacher empowerment. The conservative perspective of empowerment focuses on granting teachers new respect and *professional status*; the liberal empowerment perspective emphasizes teachers' reflective action to improve situations in the *classroom*; a critical/political perspective on empowerment encourages teachers to reflect on and confront societal and political *forces* to expand human freedom and social justice. Melenyzer's liberal perspective on empowerment is generally consistent with the orientations of shared governance principals described in our study. Common to all perspectives on empowerment defined by Melenyzer and apparent in our data as well is principals' focus on *problem solving*.

112

Schmuck and Runkel (1985) contend that problem solving is at the heart of group and organizational development. According to these authors, it is composed of the following complex elements and subskills:

- Effective communication
- Openness and trust
- The ability to gather and use action research (consistently using available feedback and data related to effectiveness of programs to *drive* collective decision making and planning)
- Conflict resolution (openly describing facts and feelings related to areas of dispute, searching for alternative solutions, committing to necessary changes, and action planning)
- Effective group decision making (characterized by open communication, a sense of interpersonal trust, the fair chance of all to influence the decision, and consensus—rather than majority, minority, or individual rule)

Highly developed groups put these elements to work in *concert* (and in a "safe" forum) to solve problems they discover in the school. As a matter of fact, a problem-solving orientation is the mark of an effective principal as well as a healthy school and staff (Blase, 1987; Blumberg & Greenfield, 1986; Leithwood & Jantzi, 1990; Lightfoot, 1983).

The Metaskill of Problem Solving

From our study, we found that shared governance principals initially *set the stage* for problem solving by helping faculty and staff members build communication-related skills and by encouraging effective procedural methods for solving problems. Just as open and honest communication is an essential prerequisite skill for problem solving, so is the ability to use a systematic approach for working through the details of a problem.

Shared governance principals encourage brainstorming, creative thinking, and a systematic approach (e.g., the Situation-Target-Path, or "STP," method discussed below) as they work with faculty and staff members to solve educational problems.

Brainstorming

An essential element in problem solving is active brainstorming. At several stages of the problem-solving enterprise shared governance principals encouraged teachers to search their minds for concepts and ideas that might be related to viable alternatives or solutions to problems. This requires rapid, uncensored, open brainstorming by a group of trusting colleagues. One of the authors, who has used brainstorming in work with shared governance schools, notes that it can effectively be done at a moment's notice because no special materials are needed. The general guidelines include the following:

1. Every idea generated is listed.
2. No discussion or criticism of ideas takes place.
3. Far-fetched ideas are encouraged because they may trigger other more practical ideas.
4. The more ideas generated the better.

Some shared governance principals used an entertaining "first experience" brainstorming exercise to sensitize faculty and staff members to the usefulness and enjoyment that come with brainstorming. Here is an example of such an exercise and directions on how to present it:

First, explain that brainstorming is a necessary and functional part of problem solving that taps the talents of many people. Then, teach brainstorming guidelines. With everyone divided into small groups and supplied with paper and markers, read the following: *Imagine you are cast ashore on a deserted island. You are nude except for a leather belt with a metal buckle. In your groups, brainstorm what can be done with the belt; see how long a list you can generate!* (You will be surprised at how creative and long the lists are.) After a few minutes of brainstorming, have group members read their lists to the large group. Re-emphasize the brainstorming guidelines and discuss how important brainstorming is for group problem solving. Encourage everyone to use brainstorming frequently.

Creative Thinking

Successful shared governance principals appear to value and support a "lateral," or creative, approach to problem solving. This is different from straight-line, "vertical," or logical analysis, in which steps or premises follow each other and build to a conclusion (de Bono, 1967). Rather, in creative thinking, all things related to the problem are considered, even those thought at first glance to be unrelated. Some people are particularly adept at "sideways" thinking, and everyone can be encouraged to explore different ways of looking at something instead of merely taking a reasonable view and proceeding logically to produce a solution. In group work, both brainstorming and creative, unusual patterns of thinking about problems can produce very promising approaches to problem solving.

A Systematic Approach:
The STP Method of Problem Solving

Analyses of our data indicated that the STP method of problem solving (adapted from Schmuck & Runkel, 1985) is consistent with the approaches taken by many shared governance teachers and principals. This approach to problem solving consists of nine steps:

1. *Identify the problem.* This step requires careful use of available data and discovery of the true *problem,* instead of a *symptom* of the problem (e.g., not "test scores are low" but "skills were not taught"; not "morale is low" but "teachers are overworked"). Identification of the problem situation (S) may cause discomfort, particularly if teachers suspect that they will be censured for existing difficulties. In such cases, principals and colleague teachers alike must emphasize the positive and hopeful aspects of problem identification. The target (T) is

where you want to go, the way you would like things to be ultimately.

2. *Generate alternate paths.* Through the use of brainstorming and creative thinking, list possible ways to address a problem.

3. *List helping and hindering forces.* Consider those factors that may serve to help (support) or hinder (inhibit) the implementation of each alternative listed in Step 2. For example, the availability of funds helps support the alternative of sponsoring a staff development session to help teachers expand their skills.

4. *Create ways to enhance or limit forces.* The helping and hindering forces listed in Step 3 can usually be strengthened (in the case of helping forces) or reduced (in the case of hindering forces). For example, it may be possible to enhance the availability of staff development funds by writing a grant proposal, appealing to the staff development director, or diverting funds from other projects.

5. *Choose action steps.* Given all the information and brainstorming completed thus far, the group chooses the most appropriate path (P) for solving the problem. This is put into an *action plan* that specifies what is done, when, by whom, and how.

6. *Anticipate problems.* Often overlooked, this step can save many heartaches. Before embarking on the action plan, potential problems (and viable alternative ways of handling them or changing the plan) must be anticipated.

7. *Act.* With group agreement and interpersonal support, the plan should be implemented.

8. *Monitor.* At every step in the plan, activities and consequences should be monitored. Adjustments or modifications should be made as necessary.

9. *Evaluate.* All problem-solving projects should be carefully evaluated, so as to improve working relationships and the effectiveness of future efforts. Openness in discussions is essential!

Shared Governance
Principals' Problem-Solving Skills

Besides using effective procedural methods for solving problems, successful shared governance principals described by teachers exhibited two primary characteristics related to solving problems: They encouraged and listened to individual input, and they made themselves available to help in problem-solving situations.

Encouraging and Listening to Individual Input

Most central to the empowerment process, from the teachers' standpoint, was shared governance principals' ability to listen to input and consistently maintain an open attitude, as the following comments reflect (all emphases added throughout):

> She is so supportive of the teachers and their ability to make good decisions. She listens to us and values our opinion, *not claiming to have all the answers.*

> The principal allows me to *speak openly and honestly.* Unlike my other experiences with principals, he hears and listens to what I have to say.

> As a professional I feel that sometimes I have ideas that may benefit the program at our school, and when this occurs, the principal *is willing to provide an audience for those ideas* and *give appropriate recognition* if the ideas are implemented.

Beyond this, principals would "often ask people individually what they think about certain issues," thus seeking out the expertise and advice of the teachers whom they respected and considered knowledgeable professionals:

> My principal believes that teachers' opinions and suggestions should be *seriously considered.*

She maintains an open-door policy. She is never "too busy" to talk with the classroom teacher. It makes me feel *my ideas or comments are important* enough to be shared with her at any time.

He listens to our ideas and acts on them if at all possible. We have been complaining about exam schedules—several people thought we could do a better one. This semester we are trying a new schedule. I feel that I can decide (along with my peers) what works or doesn't work. The principal *doesn't ever say "That won't work."* That's it for us: we have input.

Such behaviors on the part of the principal are critical to facilitating informal input processes throughout a school.

We also found that teachers have three important responses to principals who seek their input: They believe that the principal trusts them, that the principal recognizes the value of their input, and that they have freedom from reprisals when things do not go exactly as planned. Teachers' sense of empowerment was further enhanced because shared governance principals *vigorously* encouraged input from individual teachers on a *variety* of important schoolwide and classroom issues.

Furthermore, shared governance principals listened to teachers' input *even when their own opinions differed* and when changes were not possible:

He really listens. He solicits the opinions of others and really means it. If his opinion differs from mine, he really will admit that my opinion is better. Or he will stick to his; that's okay, too. Empowerment means that I can have input on decisions that affect me or my school.

She listens to what I am saying. I mean that she hears how I feel and even my frustration, as well as any suggestions I might offer for changing. *Even when she is unable to change* the policy, rule, or procedure, she *hears my frustration* and that in itself is a help. Sometimes it causes me to see things in a new way and feel in control.

Shared governance principals also listened nonjudgmentally:

> She values my opinions and ideas and allows me to share
> them with her without fear of reprisal or criticism even
> when our opinions differ.

Being Available to Help in Problem Solving

As noted above, shared governance principals' willingness to
provide advice and to be "fair and listen respectfully" greatly helped
facilitate teachers' ability to deal effectively with problems. Principals were especially helpful to teachers who dealt with student- and
parent-related conflicts; they offered sound advice and often made
themselves available to serve in mediational roles:

> When teachers have a problem with students, our principal
> is *always there* to listen and help resolve the situation. Her
> advice is always appropriate and it helps relax the teacher
> and the situation.

Furthermore, successful shared governance principals consistently
"backed" teachers in disputes with parents:

> Any time a parent has a grievance with me I feel confident
> in taking the parent to the principal. I know he will *listen
> and be supportive* of my decisions.

In the course of dealing with problems, principals tended to demonstrate "continued respect for and confidence" in teachers' judgments and actions:

> If I had a problem I know he would *understand and support
> me.* I can even make a mistake without fear of emotional
> retaliation.

As noted earlier, principals' respect and confidence were often
extended to the personal realm; teachers sensed the concern and
caring of their principals at times when they faced personal challenges.

Teachers' Reactions

Teachers in our study reported that the degree and quality of their general involvement in shared governance processes, especially in developing skills to solve problems, were strongly linked to enhanced *personal confidence*:

> The principal's commitment to site-based problem solving and his openness to innovative teaching contribute greatly to my sense of empowerment. Through our leadership team and faculty liaison groups I have an impact on administrative decisions that affect our school. *I feel self-confident.*

> My principal asks for teachers to volunteer to serve on innovative committees. She does not pick her committee members nor does she sit in on the meetings. Often, she will have a problem, turn it over to the committee, and accept whatever we come up with. *I feel valued, respected, confident, and capable. I act confidently.*

Confidence in their work encouraged teachers to solve individual classroom problems:

> He allows each teacher to develop his own style for teaching and he allows for individual differences. He does not monitor classroom activities constantly or demand detailed and extensive plans and reports from the faculty. . . . *I solve my own problems. . . . I feel more confident because of [this].*

> If I as an individual or team of teachers want to try something new, she is interested in helping us attain it. I know that I can count on her support. *I go forward with more self-confidence, ready to try new things.*

> She gave us a sense of trust. She gave us many responsibilities and decisions. We felt that she believed in us and knew we could professionally handle classroom situations. *It makes me feel confident and gives me a freedom to grow and try new things.*

Finally, in jubilant words, teachers described the feelings derived from the sense that their principal *believes* in their ability to solve classroom and schoolwide problems:

> The principal always felt we could handle problems and solve them! We, in turn, felt we could solve problems of the school. We felt *in control, part of the school.* We were always thinking of improving our school. We acted on problems and solved them without concerning the principal.

> Our principal's belief and support that his staff is made up of professionals really makes me feel supported. This quality makes one feel as if they *have the power to make choices.* My feelings are often very positive when I am empowered.

Helpful Reminders

Problem solving is the highest order skill of a team of educational colleagues. As you strive to set the stage, to use effective processes, and to exhibit supportive behaviors in problem-solving endeavors, the following reminders may be helpful.

1. Listen.

Demonstrate your trust, respect, and confidence in teachers by listening attentively to their concerns and suggestions. Often, the best solution to a problem is within the faculty members who are closest to the problem or in a seemingly unlikely place. Moreover, in finding solid solutions to problems, you will be expressing your faith in teachers as professionals.

2. Make yourself available.

One approach to availability has been called *managing by wandering around* (Peters & Waterman, 1983), in which a leader is available by frequently being on-site where the work of the organization is done. In this way, information is gained, teachers have an opportunity to interact with the principal, and many problems can be solved on the spot. This will be perceived as *sincere interest* in the work of teachers, rather than *"snoop"ervision.*

3. Teach problem-solving skills.

The skill of solving problems is not learned by osmosis, nor is it known by some miraculous method. It takes work and time in formal staff development sessions for people to learn the skills and attitudes necessary for problem solving. Set aside time for such sessions and review these skills periodically. Within these sessions, encourage brainstorming, creative thinking, and problem-solving methods.

4. Actively demonstrate your faith and confidence in teachers.

Every day, with each teacher you meet, strive to demonstrate your confidence and faith. Encourage teachers to fulfill their potential, and you will be surprised at the results; high expectations have high yield.

5. Strive to bring teachers into discussions about the overarching metaproblems of the school.

Teachers need to go beyond basic instructional questions to issues of morality and ethics as they adopt and implement programs. Questions related to the basic democratic premises on which our schools are founded need to be explored by all in the educational enterprise. Involve teachers in such discussions and then find ways that you can move together in the desired direction.

6. Be prepared to move from problem solving to problem posing.

As teachers develop their professional skills, they will move away from rational processes of choosing among possibilities to *debate* about the nature of their decisions, the ends of their efforts, and the means of achieving those ends. Thereby, in problem posing, knowledge is viewed differently and the complexity of social problems is acknowledged (Smyth, 1990). Such discussion constitutes exciting challenges for professional educators.

7. Embrace a "new paradigm" of school operation.

Quoting the words of a principal, one teacher summarized this important point:

> The principal cannot redefine education. It will take the *collective* wisdom of all educators in the school to transform the institution, and shared governance is a prerequisite *catalyst* for the revolutionary changes which will be needed to accomplish the task.

References

Blase, J. (1987). Dimensions of effective school leadership: The teachers' perspective. *American Educational Research Journal, 24*(4), 598-610.

Blumberg, A., & Greenfield, W. (1986). *The effective principal: Perspectives on school leadership* (2nd ed.). Boston: Allyn & Bacon.

de Bono, E. (1967). *New think: The use of lateral thinking in the generation of new ideas.* New York: Basic Books.

Leithwood, K., & Jantzi, D. (1990, April). *Transformational leadership: How principals can help reform school cultures.* Paper presented at the annual meeting of the American Educational Research Association, Boston.

Lightfoot, S. L. (1983). *The good high school: Portraits of character and culture.* New York: Basic Books.

Melenyzer, B. J. (1990, November). *Teacher empowerment: The discourse, meanings, and social actions of teachers.* Paper presented at the annual conference of the National Council of States on Inservice Education, Orlando, FL.

Peters, T., & Waterman, R. (1983). *In search of excellence: Lessons from America's best-run companies.* New York: Warner Books.

Schmuck, R. A., & Runkel, P. J. (1985). *The handbook of organization development in schools* (3rd ed.). Palo Alto, CA: Mayfield.

Smyth, J. (1990, April). *A pedagogical and educative view of leadership.* Paper presented at the annual meeting of the American Educational Research Association, Boston.

10

Providing Leadership
That Is Facilitative and Democratic

I find most promising those paths to empowerment that call for
a major transformation of the teacher's role.

—Sprague (1992), p. 198

Those who seek to restructure schools believe that extensive
improvement is imperative. They tend to be more aware than
others of the shortcomings, failures, and inequities of schooling,
and they are determined to bring about improvements. Hence
they are impatient with pseudo-reform and its symbolic politics.
They are apt to be in sympathy with a number of the particular
changes proposed by incremental reformers—but they hold little
hope of seeing such changes realized without broader, more
extensive, and more fundamental change.

—Raywid (1990), p. 143

In this book we have described the facilitative-democratic strategies
that teachers in our study associate with successful principal leadership in shared governance schools. Through the teachers' own words,
we have offered descriptions of the strategies used by empowering
leaders; each strategy was then explicated by reporting principals'
specific practices. For example, the strategy of *encouraging autonomy
and innovation* included the specific practices of promoting teacher
decisional authority vis-à-vis classroom instructional matters, student

control matters, and needs determinations; soliciting teacher advice; extending tangible and intangible support for individual and team experimentation; viewing failure as an opportunity to learn; and emphasizing positive elements of improvement efforts. Practices associated with *supporting risk and diminishing threat* included openly sharing information, facilitating a problem-solving approach, providing feedback, trusting teachers, and exhibiting indirect/subtle leadership behaviors. Another strategy, *establishing trust*, included such practices as encouraging openness, facilitating effective communication, modeling understanding, providing opportunities for practice of interaction skills, accepting and reducing conflict, and supporting teacher-leaders.

According to our data, principals' strategies significantly affected teachers' behavior, thinking, and attitudes. For example, the principals' encouragement of autonomy and innovation enhanced teachers' self-esteem, confidence, professional satisfaction, creativity, sense of classroom efficacy, and ability to reflect on instructional issues. Conceptually speaking, the strategies used by shared governance principals affected three dimensions of teacher empowerment:

- The *affective* dimension: teacher satisfaction, motivation, esteem, confidence, security, sense of inclusion, identification with the group and its work (sense of "we")
- The *classroom* dimension: innovation, creativity, reflection, autonomy, individualization of instruction, professional growth, classroom efficacy
- The *schoolwide* dimension: expression, ownership, commitment, sense of team, and schoolwide efficacy

In each chapter we have described only those strategies and practices that emerged directly from our data; in essence, the portrait of successful facilitative-democratic leadership was drawn entirely from reports made by empowered teachers working in shared governance schools. To date, no research has been published focusing on strategies that principals use to empower teachers and the specific effects of such strategies on teachers' sense of empowerment.

In summary, our study data argue that teachers' sense of empowerment is enhanced by the following actions of principals:

- Modeling, building, and persistently supporting an environment of trust among teachers, whom they consider professionals and experts
- Systematically structuring the school to encourage authentic collaboration by establishing readiness and common goals and by responding to the school's unique characteristics
- Supporting shared governance efforts by providing professional development and basic resources
- Supporting teacher experimentation and innovation, granting professional autonomy, and viewing failure as an opportunity to learn
- Modeling professional behavior, especially by exhibiting caring, optimism, honesty, friendliness, and enthusiasm
- Encouraging risk taking and minimizing threat (or constraints on teacher freedom and growth)
- Praising teachers and using other symbolic rewards (e.g., valuing and respecting teachers)
- Setting the stage for discussing and solving the metaproblems of a school through effective communication, openness and trust, use of action research, group participation in decision making, and the use of effective procedural methods for solving problems

Each of the principals described by teachers in our study used all of the strategies identified with facilitative-democratic leadership (in varying degrees), and teachers viewed this approach as making the major contribution to their sense of empowerment. These principals also carefully attended to and effectively balanced the psychological, social, and everyday political dimensions of their own role with those of teachers.

In the closing pages of each chapter we presented suggestions for practice related to each successful facilitative strategy. These suggestions are not intended to be "formulas" for effective facilitative leadership; rather, readers should consider the appropriateness of each suggestion in light of the unique context and limitations of their school and staff. We further noted that teachers were highly resentful of and resistant to former principals who found open discussion about problems to be threatening.

The findings of our study echo those of other research on leadership in shared governance schools. These findings confirm the critical role that principals play in initiating and facilitating change for instructional leadership and for managing group process (Lindle, 1992; Mills, 1990; Osterman, 1989; Schmuck & Runkel, 1985). However, little is known about the characteristics of successful practice in more varied settings and at different stages in the development and implementation of shared governance processes. Indeed, because schools are idiosyncratic in nature and each has its unique needs, goals, and personnel, it is not possible to develop a general theory of facilitative-democratic leadership that would be specifically applicable to all cases.

How, then, can a principal who is genuinely committed to democratic principles and procedures know when to use the facilitative strategies described by respondents in our study? Aspiring shared governance principals may find the following questions helpful in thinking about their leadership approach:

1. Do I think of teachers as coleaders?
2. What specific characteristics of our school, its staff, and our community might facilitate or hinder the initiation and implementation of shared governance?
3. What constraints to shared governance exist in our school district?
4. What is the readiness status of our faculty and staff to engage in collegial decision making about agreed-on goals?
5. Do teachers in our school regularly seek and offer help, support, and advice about their teaching among themselves? Are there opportunities for such help among colleagues?
6. Which of the facilitative-democratic leadership strategies would be effective in working with our teachers?
7. What implications for future hiring exist in this approach?

We now know that attempts to restructure schools (e.g., site-based management, participative decision making, decentralization, re-structuring, or shared governance) have, for the most part, resulted in only "partial" development of successful democratic structures and processes. In fact, the ideal of school-level decision making has been constrained not only by bureaucracy, tradition, and school context but also by administrators' and teachers' own discomfort with radically different roles (Weiss, 1990). An important question for aspiring democratic principals is this: *How prepared am I* to enact a dramatically different role, one of shared responsibility and authority with teachers?

Assumptions of Facilitative-Democratic Leadership

What constitutes successful facilitative-democratic leadership? What behaviors, goals, and purposes will transform bureaucratic schools into shared governance schools? The knowledge gleaned from teachers involved in our study and from the empirical and "popular" literature leads us to several *fundamental assumptions* about facilitative leadership in democratic schools.

First, the role of the principal becomes primarily that of facilitat-ing collaborative efforts among mutually supportive, trusting pro-fessionals. Thus the school is a learning community in which *leaders become teachers* and *teachers become leaders*. Facilitation consists largely of providing resources and opportunities for examination of data gathered by action research and ensuring that opportunities exist for collective determination of goals and objectives. Foster (1986) expands on the theme of leaders becoming teachers and teachers becoming leaders:

Leadership can spring from anywhere; it is not a quality that comes with an office or a person. Rather, it derives from the context and ideas of individuals who influence each other. Thus, a principal may at times be a leader and at other times, a follower. A teacher may be a leader, and the principal a follower. Leadership is an act bounded in space and time; it

is an act that enables others and allows them, in turn, to become enablers. (p. 187)

A second assumption about leadership in shared governance
schools is that the leader helps others recognize the complexities of
schools as social organizations set in myriad contexts. Thus the
approach to facilitative-democratic leadership in any school must
be tailored to that particular school. Such leadership can be shaped
by an understanding of the general strategies described in this book,
but ultimately it rests on the particular needs and purposes determined by the evolving collective leadership of the specific school.

A final assumption about successful leadership in shared governance schools is that constraining forces (e.g., lack of support or
mandates from the district office, opposition to alternative governance designs) must be minimized or eliminated. The bureaucratic
nature and conservative culture of traditional schools create difficulties for the development of a new form of democratic governance. For example, bureaucratic structures consistently demand
evaluation, accountability, and conformity to regulations. Those
involved in shared governance must often obtain "waivers" to enact
essential changes. Consequently, democratic, creative alternatives
become problematic.[1]

Shared governance leaders must negotiate a viable solution to
the problem of bureaucratic intrusion (whether it results from reasonable structures or from administrative paraphernalia). In effect,
each leader must confront sensitive questions: How far can shared
governance go? To what extent will educators be involved in substantive schoolwide decision making?

"Moving" Schools Versus "Stuck" Schools

Using both quantitative and qualitative research strategies,
Rosenholtz (1989) described "moving" schools as those in which
teachers have a common purpose and work openly and cooperatively.
In "stuck" schools, on the other hand, teachers feel no sense of progress
or growth and tend to have lower aspirations and lack motivation
to achieve. In studying the work lives of teachers Rosenholtz

noted that in the "moving" schools instructional goals and *evaluative-performance criteria were the focus of teachers* and principals. In fact, "a multitude of supportive collegial voices" led to speaking "boldly, nobly . . . to create . . . beginnings instead of endings"; teachers were "welded . . . into one common voice" (pp. 206-207).

Rosenholtz's teachers believed, as did those in our study, that teaching is important, that alternative practices might improve their efforts, that peers are resources, that a sense of community helps teachers to persist in the face of difficulties, and that they themselves are learners and carry a spirit of continuous improvement.

In contrast, teachers in "stuck" or low-consensus schools lacked a sense of community. Isolation in classrooms, sparse professional dialogue, continual frustration and tedium, and random pursuit of work issues led to feelings of futility, lost ambitions, and complacency. Moreover, for want of common purpose and without shared governance among teachers, poor student conduct remained uncorrected and devoured teachers' attention and "left bitter traces and tarnished hopes as their time and energy to teach vaporized into thin air" (p. 207). Throughout her discussion, Rosenholtz remarked on the lost commitment of such teachers, which led to low investment in work as well as other negative impacts:

> teachers' frustration with principals, students, and parents, which left them only a residue of collective resentment and despair; in their lack of nourishment from colleagues, which consumed their inner resources that in their entry to the profession had once inspired high aspirations and promise; and in the absence of professional growth, which stunted their anticipation of new teaching challenges and possibilities. (p. 149)

Isolated settings, whether they derive from the influence of restrictive, bureaucratic district offices or from conditions within a given school, compel teachers in the direction of self-reliance. In such settings, peer assistance and collaboration violate school norms, and the benefits of mutual assistance and colleagues' special skills are ignored. Thus problem solving through reasoning, debating, and discussing is hindered. **At least initially, it is the principal's (i.e.,**

the leader's) responsibility to encourage and provide the necessary conditions for collegial interaction to flourish.

Necessary Conditions
for Facilitative-Democratic Leadership

Empowerment means more than simply "allowing" teachers
access to decision making. In fact, principals must relinquish, delegate,
or share *power* as well as responsibility, thus "transforming followers
into leaders" (Burns, 1978). Furthermore, successful shared governance principals are not "laissez-faire" types or "shrinking violets."
To the contrary, they honestly share their *own* opinions and actively
engage in discussion and debate. For these principals, day-to-day
functioning as a facilitative-democratic leader involves the following:

- Developing teachers' skills to gather data, make decisions, and
  solve problems (see Kirby, 1991, for a discussion of related prop-
  ositions). Specifically, action research in support of collaborative inquiry—educators becoming "critical friends" to each
  other—is considered a powerful tool for improving schools,
  but it does not negate the need for leadership to establish
  collegial respect and support for the work of teachers.
- Freely engaging in critical discourse in which educators discuss, debate, and dialogue—wherein the best argument wins
- Recognizing teachers as subject and pedagogical experts
- Involving parents and other citizens in providing a legislative
  framework for schooling that supports democratic processes
- Involving oneself as a peer and equal with teachers in the
  educational enterprise

In sum, highly successful, shared governance principals
know it is not power over people and events that counts
but, rather, power over accomplishments and over the
achievement of organizational purposes. They understand
that teachers need to be empowered to act—to be given
the necessary responsibility that releases their potential

and makes their actions and decisions count. (Sergiovanni, 1987, p. 121)

Shared governance principals involve everyone in the educational enterprise and consider themselves one among many equally important persons in the decision-making effort. They see teacher participation as a *right,* not a *gift,* and they take the approach that all teachers are leaders.

A Right or a Gift?

In *Bringing Out the Best in Teachers,* Blase and Kirby (1992) described the leadership orientation of open and effective principals working in traditional school settings. This book, in contrast, describes the work of successful principals in schools implementing shared governance principles. In both studies the researchers found that principals ameliorated the constraints of bureaucracy by motivating teachers' work through means both tangible (e.g., funds, time, materials) and intangible (e.g., authority, autonomy, respect, trust) and by displaying supportive personal characteristics (e.g., honesty, caring).

Both studies indicated that principals focused on motivating teachers to achieve instructional goals. *However, shared governance principals' commitment to using facilitative strategies to empower teachers was far more extensive.* Thus teachers tended to view participation as a "right," not a "gift." It was also evident, however, that neither open/effective traditional principals nor successful shared governance principals attempted to achieve an emancipatory orientation to empowerment. In such an orientation, teachers actively apply knowledge of the historical, economical, political, and cultural contexts of education to challenge societal and institutional arrangements that prevent achieving social justice, social equality, and social democracy (McLaren, 1988).

This finding raises several questions: What factors inhibit the development of a fully democratic/emancipatory perspective on empowerment? How can principals overcome such limitations? What are the related implications for teacher and principal preparation? Although pursuit of these issues is beyond the scope of this book, we recognize their significance in terms of democratic functioning in schools.

A second distinction between the open/effective principals described by Blase and Kirby (1992) and the shared governance principals discussed in this book is captured by the notion of transformational leadership (Burns, 1978). Burns viewed transformational leaders as fundamentally moral: Their leadership emerges from the needs, aspirations, and values of followers and results in mutuality of purpose between themselves and followers. Moreover, followers can make choices among real alternatives. "Such leadership occurs when . . . persons engage with others in such a way that leaders and followers raise each other to higher levels of motivation and morality" (p. 20). Rather than awarding teachers the "gift" of participation, transformational leaders engage *with* teachers to define both the means and ends of human action:

> The essence of leadership . . . is the recognition of real need, the uncovering and exploiting of contradictions among values and between values and practice, and the realigning of values . . . and the governance of change. Essentially, the leader's task is consciousness-raising on a wide plane. (pp. 43-44)

To further complicate matters, principals' attempts to juggle legal responsibilities with efforts to diminish or dismantle the existing hierarchy may be disturbing to teachers. This situation may also produce confusion when teachers are trying to exercise their rights. Moreover, principals may experience ambivalence as they forge democratic communities (see Bredeson, 1993, for a detailed discussion of the anxieties, disturbances, and role strain, such as fear of failure, loss of identity, and loss of control, plaguing principals as they work with newly empowered colleagues). The implications of these difficulties are clear:

- District support for nascent attempts at shared governance is a necessity.

- Teachers must grow beyond accepting the "gift" of shared governance to seeking (even demanding) their *right* as experts to participate in decisions as well as embracing responsibilities.
- Shared governance is evolutionary; we do not yet know what might happen if shared governance approaches become mandated by *policy*. Will teachers be satisfied? What will be the effect on teacher involvement and decision making?

Teachers as Leaders: Creating Power in a Community of Leaders

Unfortunately, the reality of life in schools is that teachers' work is often deskilled and that teachers are frequently devalued and diverted from their cause. Consequently, they may engage in *defensive teaching* and "bracket [or ignore] their personal knowledge [which] heightens the feeling . . . that schooling is a ritual rather than an education" (McNeil, 1986, p. 215). Furthermore, as rather loosely coupled organizations (Weick, 1976), schools have developed into organizations in which administrators and teachers work separately and independently. In contrast, shared governance principals, according to our study, see themselves as *academic* leaders; they are invested in instructional matters and *consider all teachers as leaders and themselves as colleague-teachers.*

Much research has indicated that teachers desire more formal "power," or freedom to use professional discretion as they work with other teachers (Lieberman, 1988; Maeroff, 1988). That is, teachers want the authority to make "final" decisions in the classroom and in the school, individually and collectively, with other teachers and administrators.

Bacharach and Lawler (1980), Conley (1991), and Tate (1991) provide an understanding of the distinctions among power, authority, influence, and control. The outcomes of principals' power behavior are discussed by Kshensky and Muth (1991), who note that influence brings willing acceptance, authority brings obedience, and coercion brings capitulation (p. 18).

In our study, we found that shared governance principals included teachers in decisions that expanded their influence in the classroom, the school, and even the district within district-imposed limitations. Such decisions related to personnel, time, space, students, and the "stuff" of learning (materials and curricula). Teachers, for example, were actively involved in all schoolwide instructional matters, as well as in hiring, budgeting, student distribution/placement, and planning matters.

Successful shared governance principals know that greater participation in decision making yields greater productivity, job satisfaction, and organizational commitment (Rice & Schneider, 1992). Our findings also suggest that shared governance principals *enable others to become leaders*. Indeed, "the best principals are not heroes; they are hero-makers" (Barth, 1988, p. 146). Furthermore, it appears that shared governance principals create a community of leaders that offers independence, interdependence, and resourcefulness:

> A community of leaders is a vision of what might become a condition of the school culture, a part of the shared norms, beliefs, rituals, and actions of the school. And a community of leaders is far more than a piece of a professional school culture. Without shared leadership it is not possible for a professional culture to exist. Professionalism and shared leadership are one and the same. (Barth, 1988, pp. 146-147)

To be sure, developing teacher leadership skills requires specialized training programs, which principals will need to provide. Within this work, the "gains and strains" that derive from introducing teacher leadership (with its attendant shifts in roles and authority) will be noticed (Little, 1988).

Moving Toward Greater Facilitative-Democratic Leadership and Teacher Empowerment

In dissolving present bureaucratic structures, principals who wish to pursue a fully facilitative-democratic form of leadership will not merely empower teachers from outside—"Am *I* going to empower *you!*" (Bredo, 1991, p. 3). Rather, they will support teachers who *empower themselves* through reflective and political actions that mirror their claims to expertise about instructional matters. Empowerment is thus naturally—as opposed to officially—achieved.

Sharing authority as well as responsibility more fully with teachers across roles and hierarchical levels will create schools and systems that look very different from those of this century. In these schools, a community of learners respect and trust each other, draw on each other's many talents, and enact their passion for teaching. However, establishing these schools requires people who have appropriate preservice and in-service education that produces the attitudes of a reflective practitioner and child advocate (Barth, 1988) as well as a politically active professional. Empowered teachers can help create such schools by serving as clinical supervisors for teachers-in-training, mentoring new teachers, serving on state certification task forces, influencing hiring and placement decisions, and collaborating with university professionals to improve preparation and in-service education.

In looking at empowerment in relation to other reform ideas within the rhetoric of the "second wave" of school reform, Tate's (1991) definition of teacher empowerment is consistent with a more advanced form of facilitative-democratic leadership. He defines teacher empowerment as "the broadening of teachers' expert and professional authority over schooling" (p. 3). Implications of this definition of teacher empowerment include the following ideas:

- Teachers are the *experts* on teaching, hence their enhanced role (decentralization).
- Teachers can provide *good judgments* about educational issues (professionalization).
- Empowered teaching should be characterized by *reflection and self-fulfillment* (enablement) that also extends to students.
- Empowerment is a *democratic* reform that yields broadened participation (democratization).

- Empowerment is a *bottom-up* as well as a top-down reform (inversion of the hierarchy, with teachers reclaiming their right to have a say in policies affecting them). (Tate, 1991, pp. 1-6)

Maxcy's (1991) conception of empowerment, which includes rational authority or teacher expertise, teacher collaboration and collegiality, and the democratic culture or climate of the school, is similar to Tate's conception and emphasizes the importance of teachers as the real catalysts for change (Maeroff, 1988).

In considering the future of teacher empowerment, we might expand the notion to recognize that *power* comes from three levels: the individual level (through self-efficacy, that is, political skill, expertise, and internal/external locus of control), the group level (through interpersonal relations and coalitions formed by social or professional/collegial respect and support), and the organizational level (through attaining certain roles within the school and classroom) (Lee, Smith, & Cioci, 1993). This suggests that principals can encourage and support the expansion of power for each teacher, each group operating in the school, and the school as a whole.

Future Research

As we have noted, the questions of leading, how to perform as a leader, and how leadership can be changed cannot be answered apart from a consideration of the school organization and its context. Our book cannot answer specific questions about what should happen at a particular time in a given school. It fails to reveal how successful shared governance principals balance, in concert, the myriad issues of democratic leadership.

We propose that investigators consider the potentially instructive value of intensive case studies about the experience of implementing shared governance in varying settings. Such studies would enable us to analyze variations in leadership and would provide rich and descriptive portraits of undoubtedly dramatic efforts to restructure existing educational bureaucracies and answer serious questions. (We are indebted to Carl Glickman for his thoughtful contributions to our thinking on this topic.)

A Final Thought

> Empowerment is defined as enabling teachers who have been silenced to speak; as helping them to develop a sense of agency, become challengers, and take initiatives; and as investing them with the right to participate in the determination of school goals and policies and to exercise professional judgment about what and how to teach. Critical educational scholars elaborate upon those general themes by envisioning even more powerful alternatives for teachers. (Sprague, 1992, p. 199)

Where do educators go from here? As we have seen, empowerment may occur at a level at which teachers are granted professional respect. It may be limited to classroom situations, or it may extend to a level at which teachers assume a critical and active approach as they confront forces that limit educational possibilities.

Empowerment invariably includes some frustrations and interferences (time, resistance, bureaucracy). According to some writers, empowered teachers should be *social and political activists* who will not "allow their work to be coopted and domesticated by whatever political forces dominate the school hierarchy. . . . They recognize their distinctive place in the culture and embrace an emancipatory vision, [and] begin to function as transformative intellectuals" (Sprague, 1992, p. 193). Indeed, they relentlessly pursue the "unmasking of the lies, myths and distortions that construct the basis for the dominant order" (Giroux & Freire, 1987, p. xii) so that they may change oppressive circumstances in which they find themselves. An important body of recent educational scholarship (Apple, 1988; Greene, 1988) advocates this form of teacher empowerment as well as the view that teachers are "transformative intellectuals" who ask questions and challenge current ways (Giroux, 1988; Smyth, 1987). Indeed, it is clear that true teacher empowerment and the democratization of schools is unlikely to occur unless educational leaders support such actions by teachers and aggressively collaborate with teachers and others to pursue educational goals.

Note

1. The reality of the school organization is that the education and control functions may not be as separated from each other (loosely coupled) as previously thought. *Control* goals center on routine and management of students; *educational* goals imply unpredictable outcomes among widely varying students. Teachers are at the juncture of these two conflicting goals. They are rewarded for the ability to control students (rather than their ability to teach) and their skills are trivialized. Not surprising, this situation frequently yields defensive teaching (McNeil, 1986) and a *disinclination to collaborate*. The tension between educating students and providing mechanisms of control is also reflected in the relationship between teaching practices in schools and the larger society. Such organizational contradictions inside schools often create a "boring but polite ritual of class" (McNeil, 1986, p. xix).

References

Apple, M. W. (1988). *Teachers and texts: A political economy of class and gender relations in education.* New York: Routledge.

Bacharach, S. B., & Lawler, E. J. (1980). *Power and politics in organizations.* San Francisco: Jossey-Bass.

Barth, R. S. (1988). School. A community of leaders. In A. Lieberman (Ed.), *Building a professional culture in schools* (pp. 129-147). New York: Teachers College Press.

Blase, J., & Kirby, P. C. (1992). *Bringing out the best in teachers: What effective principals do.* Newbury Park, CA: Corwin.

Bredeson, P. V. (1993). Letting go of outlived professional identities: A study of role transition and role strain for principals in restructured schools. *Educational Administration Quarterly, 29*(1), 34-68.

Bredo, E. (1991, March). *Paradoxes of teacher empowerment: A response.* Paper presented at the annual meeting of the Philosophy of Education Society, Arlington, VA.

Burns, J. M. (1978). *Leadership.* New York: Harper & Row.

Conley, S. (1991). Review of research on teacher participation in school decision making. *Review of Research in Education, 17,* 225-266.

Foster, W. (1986). *Paradigms and promises: New approaches to educational administration.* Buffalo, NY: Prometheus.

Giroux, H. A. (1988). *Teachers as intellectuals: Toward a critical pedagogy of learning.* Granby, MA: Bergin & Garvey.

Giroux, H., & Freire, P. (1987). Series introduction. In D. Livingston & Contributors (Eds.), *Critical pedagogy and cultural power* (pp. xi-xvi). Minneapolis: University of Minnesota Press.

Greene, M. (1988). *The dialectic of freedom.* New York: Teachers College Press.

Kirby, P. C. (1991, April). *Shared decision making: Moving from concerns about restrooms to concerns about classrooms.* Paper presented at the annual meeting of the American Educational Research Association, Chicago.

Kshensky, M., & Muth, R. (1991, April). *The mutual empowerment of teachers and principals.* Paper presented at the annual meeting of the American Educational Research Association, Chicago.

Lee, V. E., Smith, J. B., & Cioci, M. (1993). Teachers and principals: Gender-related perceptions of leadership and power in secondary schools. *Educational Evaluation and Policy Analysis, 15*(2), 153-180.

Lieberman, A. (Ed.). (1988). *Building a professional culture in schools.* New York: Teachers College Press.

Lindle, J. C. (1992, April). *The effects of shared decision-making on instructional leadership: Case studies of the principal.* Paper presented at the annual meeting of the American Educational Research Association, San Francisco.

Little, J. W. (1988). Assessing the prospects for teacher leadership. In A. Lieberman (Ed.), *Building a professional culture in schools* (pp. 78-106). New York: Teachers College Press.

Maeroff, G. (1988). *The empowerment of teachers: Overcoming the crisis of confidence.* New York: Teachers College Press.

Maxcy, S. J. (1991). *Educational leadership: A critical pragmatic perspective.* New York: Bergin & Garvey.

McLaren, P. (1988). Language, social structure and production of subjectivity. *Critical Pedagogy Networkers, 1*(2-3), 1-10.

McNeil, L. M. (1986). *Contradictions of control: School structure and school knowledge.* London: Routledge.

Mills, G. E. (1990). *A consumer's guide to school improvement* (Trends and Issues series, No. 4). Eugene, OR: ERIC Clearing House on Educational Management. (ERIC Document Reproduction Service No. ED 313 800)

Osterman, K. P. (1989, April). *Supervision and shared authority: A study of principal and teacher control in six urban schools.* Paper presented at the annual meeting of the American Educational Research Association, San Francisco.

Raywid, M. (1990). The evolving effort to improve schools: Pseudo-reform, incremental reform, and restructuring. *Phi Delta Kappan, 72*(2), 139-143.

Rice, E. M., & Schneider, G. T. (1992, April). *A decade of teacher empowerment: An empirical analysis of teacher involvement in decision making.* Paper presented at the annual meeting of the American Educational Research Association, San Francisco.

Rosenholtz, S. J. (1989). *Teachers' workplace: The social organization of schools.* New York: Longman.

Schmuck, R. A., & Runkel, P. J. (1985). *The handbook of organizational development in schools.* Palo Alto, CA: Mayfield.

Sergiovanni, T. J. (1987). The theoretical bases for cultural leadership. In L. T. Sheive & M. B. Schoenheit (Eds.), *Leadership: Examining the elusive* (pp. 116-129). Alexandria, VA: Association for Supervision and Curriculum Development.

Smyth, J. (1987). Transforming teaching through intellectualizing the work of teachers. In J. Smyth (Ed.), *Educating teachers: Changing the nature of pedagogical knowledge* (pp. 155-168). London: Falmer.

Sprague, J. (1992). Critical perspectives on teacher empowerment. *Communication Education, 41*(2), 181-203.

Tate, P. M. (1991, April). *A resource allocation perspective on teacher empowerment.* Paper presented at the annual meeting of the American Educational Research Association, Chicago.

Weick, K. (1976). Educational organizations as loosely coupled systems. *Administrative Science Quarterly, 21,* 1-19.

Weiss, C. (1990, April). *How much shared leadership is there in public high schools?* Paper presented at the annual meeting of the American Educational Research Association, Boston.

Resource A

RESEARCH METHOD
AND PROCEDURES

This book has emphasized the practical aspects of leadership in shared governance schools. Yet some readers may be interested in understanding the method and procedures used to produce the data on which the book is based. For those readers, a description is provided below.

Data collection and analysis were consistent with symbolic interactionist theory. Although this theoretical approach recognizes that structural factors influence action, it emphasizes the meanings that people assign to action. In other words, people's reflexivity is given more importance than structural factors. As a product of social action, the individual is influenced by but maintains sufficient distance from others and is capable of initiating individual action (Blumer, 1969; Mead, 1934). Symbolic interactionism, in contrast to some qualitative research orientations, stresses individual perception and interpretation (Blumer, 1969; Tesch, 1988).

Therefore, the study reported in this book used open-ended questions and investigated the following broad question: How do teachers perceive the characteristics of school principals that influence their sense of empowerment? The importance of perceptual data to studies focusing on influence is well established (Bacharach & Lawler, 1980; Ball, 1987; Blase, 1991b; Hamilton & Biggart, 1985; Mangham, 1979; Pfeffer, 1981). In fact, with few exceptions, published studies of this kind in education have relied heavily on data regarding the perspectives of actors at the school level.

Typically, studies of influence have focused on the "strategies" used by individuals and groups to achieve their goals in organizational settings. However, such approaches are somewhat limited because they emphasize only "lines of action" (Lofland, 1976, p. 42) that are considered intentional and goal directed. Theoretically, "any action, consciously or unconsciously motivated, may have . . . significance in a given situation" (Blase, 1991a, p. 11), depending on people's perceptions (Bachrach & Baratz, 1962; French & Raven, 1959; Galbraith, 1983; Goffman, 1972; Hall, 1972; Hardy, 1987; Kriesberg, 1973; Lukes, 1974). Therefore, it was decided to examine broadly and inclusively the "characteristics" of principals that teachers perceived to have significance vis-à-vis their empowerment.

Consistent with exploratory-inductive approaches to qualitative inquiry, no a priori categories were used to direct data collection. Instead, perceptual data were collected and analyzed to generate descriptive categories, themes, and conceptual and theoretical ideas (Bogdan & Biklen, 1982; Bogdan & Taylor, 1975; Glaser, 1978; Glaser & Strauss, 1967).

Successful principals were identified through the use of League criteria (educational focus, governance processes, use of action research), annual reports, on-site visitations, teacher reports, and reports of facilitators (League staff members assigned to the school). Only those principals considered *highly successful* were studied.

Allport (1942) has argued that an open-ended questionnaire is considered a personal document in qualitative research that investigates a person's subjective perspectives. Such a questionnaire is defined as any self-revealing document that intentionally or unintentionally yields information regarding the structure, dynamics, and functioning of the author's life (p. xii). Accordingly, a questionnaire is a personal document when research participants have substantial control over the content of their responses.

Although questionnaires like this have been used successfully in other recent research (Blase, 1986, 1988, 1993; Blase & Pajak, 1986), it should be noted that the study reported here focuses on perceptual data relevant to teachers' perspectives of principals' characteristics. The consistency of teachers' perceptions, for instance, in relation to principals' perceptions, cannot be demonstrated here. In fact, symbolic interaction theory would argue that the perspectives of others would vary (Blumer, 1969; Bogdan & Taylor, 1975; Mead, 1934).

The Inventory of Principals' Characteristics that Contribute to Teacher Empowerment (IPCCTE), an open-ended questionnaire, was constructed to collect personal meanings on the study topic. An initial version of the questionnaire was developed in consultation with professors and a group of six teachers. This instrument was pilot-tested with 27 full-time teachers who were graduate students at a major university in the southwestern United States. Suggestions made by both groups were used to design the final form of the instrument.

Besides a cover page introducing the research topic, the IPCCTE consists of three legal-size pages for completion. On the first of these pages, teachers are asked to give background information and rate their principal with regard to overall contribution to their sense of empowerment on a sliding scale from 1 to 7. The question that appeared on the IPCCTE was "Of all the things in the school that may/could contribute to your sense of empowerment, how much do characteristics of your principal (e.g., behavior, attitudes, values, goals, etc.) contribute?" (The mean score for principals' overall influence was 6.1.) On pages 3 and 4 of the questionnaire, teachers are asked to provide detailed descriptions of *two* characteristics (one on each page) of their principals (e.g., attitude, behavior, value, etc.) that influence their empowerment. The following items appear on page 3 and are repeated on page 4:

(1) Describe one *characteristic* (attitude, value, behavior, etc.) of your principal that contributes to your sense of

empowerment. Please illustrate this characteristic by describing real-life examples of it below.

(2) Please explain *why* this characteristic makes you feel empowered. Again, give real examples to illustrate why.

(3) To show what *you* mean by being empowered as it relates to this characteristic of your principal, please describe and give examples of *your* feelings, thoughts, and behaviors. We want to know what feelings, thoughts, and behavior result.

The IPCCTE was administered to 285 teachers in a select group of 11 schools—5 elementary, 3 middle, and 3 high schools—all of which had been members of the League of Professional Schools since its inception in 1990. Teacher participation in this study was voluntary. One teacher in each of these schools administered the questionnaire to teachers during a meeting, collected completed questionnaires, and mailed them directly to a university address. School principals were not present during these meetings. Given the open-ended nature of the IPCCTE, a period of about 35 minutes was required for its completion.

As charter members of the League of Professional Schools these 11 schools each began implementing shared governance structures and action research protocols in fall 1990. The League's purpose is to establish representative, democratic decision-making structures to promote teacher involvement in school-wide instructional and curricular decisions. Governance structures often deal with topics such as staff development, educational materials, program innovation, classroom management, scheduling, budgeting, hiring, and textbook adoption. Action research involves school staff members in collecting, analyzing, and interpreting data to assess the effects of shared decision making on students, teachers, administrators, and parents and to improve decision-making processes and outcomes.

The League of Professional Schools does not specifically prescribe how member schools are to realize their commitment to shared governance. Each school is encouraged to create policies and procedures that fit its unique situation. Membership in the League provides (a) opportunities to network with other schools at periodic meetings involving teams from all League schools; (b) a biannual network exchange newsletter; (c) access to an information retrieval system to honor requests for information relevant to instructional initiatives; (d) planning, evaluation, research, and instrumentation services via telephone; and (e) a yearly on-site visit by either a League staff member, university associate, or League practitioner.

Schools interested in League membership send a team (usually three teachers and the principal) to a two-day orientation and planning workshop in which the central premises of the League—shared governance, action research—are described in the context of instructional and curricular issues. On the basis of this information, staff members of a given school vote (by secret ballot) on becoming League members. An 80% favorable vote is required before schools are eligible to join the League. Using similar voting procedures, each school decides either annually or semiannually whether it wants to continue membership in the League.

The study sample consisted of 285 teachers (59 males and 226 females) from rural ($n = 68$), suburban ($n = 183$), and urban ($n = 34$) school locations. Elementary ($n = 97$), middle ($n = 116$), and high school teachers ($n = 72$) participated. The average age of teachers was 38; the average number of years in teaching was 12. Of the sample, 213 were tenured teachers and 72 were nontenured. Married ($n = 213$), single ($n = 52$), and divorced teachers ($n = 20$) participated. Highest degrees earned were B.A./B.S. ($n = 127$), M.Ed./Ed.S. ($n = 153$), and Ed.D./Ph.D. ($n = 5$). Teachers in the 11 schools surveyed described both male ($n = 6$) and female principals ($n = 5$). The mean number of years with the principal at the time of this study was 5.

In general, very slight differences were apparent when the study sample was compared with the national distribution of teachers in terms of gender, age, marital status, highest degrees earned, average number of years in teaching, and tenure/nontenure. However, the percentages of urban and rural teachers in the sample were lower than those in the national sample, and the percentage of suburban teachers was higher. Finally, the sample had a lower proportion of elementary teachers and a higher proportion of middle/junior high school teachers. The proportion of high school teachers in the sample was consistent with what is found nationally (National Education Association, 1983, 1990).

Data from the study respondents were coded according to principles for inductive research and comparative analysis (Glaser, 1978; Glaser & Strauss, 1967). This form of analysis requires a comparison of each new unit of data to those coded previously for emergent categories and subcategories. Analysis of each questionnaire page generated 367 examples of principals' influence characteristics. Characteristics were coded into strategies (i.e., intentional, goal-directed actions) and personal characteristics. Each strategy/characteristic was then analyzed to determine its impact on aspects of teacher empowerment: feelings, thinking, and behavior (Item 3 on the IPCCTE). Display matrixes were designed to synthesize these data for each of the major strategies/characteristics (Miles & Huberman, 1984).

Study participants were asked to discuss one leadership characteristic on each of the two questionnaire pages provided for description. (Some participants used only one page and described one characteristic.) Therefore, each completed questionnaire page was coded for one characteristic only; however, respondents often identified additional characteristics in discussing a particular characteristic. The number of examples of influence characteristics derived from the data equals the number of usable pages completed.

Descriptive matrixes were also used to identify and refine conceptual and theoretical ideas derived from the data. For example, such matrixes permitted comparisons across principals' strategies and were quite helpful in refining analyses of emergent themes. This protocol also permitted comparisons of the descriptive and theoretical ideas produced by the study with the relevant extant literature (Glaser, 1978; Glaser & Strauss, 1967).

One researcher alone analyzed the entire data set. Professors, doctoral students, and teachers were consulted on a regular basis when questions arose.

Consistent with guidelines for inductive-grounded analyses, all of the descriptive, conceptual, and theoretical ideas discussed in this book were gleaned directly from data produced by the IPCCTE. Because of space limitations, only brief excerpts from the data are presented to illustrate selected ideas. Teachers often used principals' first names in their descriptions. To preserve principals' anonymity, first names have been replaced with "he" or "she" or the phrase "my principal."

References

Allport, G. (1942). *The use of personal documents in psychological science.* New York: Social Science Research Council.

Bacharach, S. B., & Lawler, E. J. (1980). *Power and politics in organizations: The social psychology of conflict, coalitions, and bargaining.* San Francisco: Jossey-Bass.

Bachrach, P., & Baratz, M. S. (1962). Two faces of power. *American Political Science Review, 56,* 947-952.

Ball, S. J. (1987). *The micro-politics of the school: Towards a theory of school organization.* London: Methuen.

Blase, J. (1986). A qualitative analysis of sources of teacher stress: Consequences for performance. *American Educational Research Journal, 23,* 13-40.

Blase, J. (1988). The everyday political perspectives of teachers: Vulnerability and conservatism. *Qualitative Studies in Education, 1*(2), 125-142.

Blase, J. (1991a). The micropolitical perspective. In J. Blase (Ed.), *The politics of life in schools: Power, conflict, and cooperation* (pp. 1-18). Newbury Park, CA: Sage.

Blase, J. (1991b). Analysis and discussion: Some concluding remarks. In J. Blase (Ed.), *The politics of life in schools: Power, conflict, and cooperation* (pp. 237-255). Newbury Park, CA: Sage.

Blase, J. (1993). The micropolitics of effective school-based leadership: Teachers' perspectives. *Educational Administration Quarterly, 29*(2), 142-163.

Blase, J., & Pajak, E. (1986). The impact of teachers' work-life on personal life: A qualitative analysis. *Alberta Journal of Educational Research, 32*(4), 307-322.

Blumer, H. (1969). *Symbolic interactionism: Perspective and method.* Englewood Cliffs, NJ: Prentice Hall.

Bogdan, R., & Biklen, S. (1982). *Qualitative research for education: An introduction to theory and methods.* Boston: Allyn & Bacon.

Bogdan, R., & Taylor, S. (1975). *Introduction to qualitative research methods: A phenomenological approach to the social sciences.* New York: John Wiley.

French, J., & Raven, B. (1959). The bases of social power. In D. Cartwright (Ed.), *Studies in social power* (pp. 150-167). Ann Arbor, MI: Institute of Social Research.

Galbraith, J. K. (1983). *The anatomy of power.* Boston: Houghton Mifflin.

Glaser, B. G. (1978). *Theoretical sensitivity: Advances in the methodology of grounded theory.* Mill Valley, CA: Sociology Press.

Glaser, B. G., & Strauss, A. L. (1967). *The discovery of grounded theory: Strategies for qualitative research.* Chicago: Aldine.

Goffman, E. (1972). *Strategic interaction: An analysis of doubt and calculation in face-to-face, day-to-day dealings with one another.* New York: Ballantine Books.

Hall, P. M. (1972). A symbolic interactionist analysis of politics. *Sociological Inquiry, 42*(3-4), 35-75.

Hamilton, G. G., & Biggart, N. W. (1985). Why people obey: Theoretical observations on power and obedience in complex organizations. *Sociological Perspectives, 28*(1), 3-28.

Hardy, C. (1987). The contribution of political science to organizational behavior. In J. W. Lorsch (Ed.), *Handbook of organizational behavior* (pp. 96-108). Englewood Cliffs, NJ: Prentice Hall.

Kriesberg, L. (1973). *The sociology of social conflicts.* Englewood Cliffs, NJ: Prentice Hall.

Lofland, J. (1976). *Doing social life: The qualitative study of human interaction in natural settings.* New York: John Wiley.

Lukes, S. (1974). *Power: A radical view.* London: Macmillan.

Mangham, I. (1979). *The politics of organizational change.* Westport, CT: Greenwood.

Mead, G. H. (1934). *Mind, self and society.* Chicago: University of Chicago Press.

Miles, M. B., & Huberman, A. M. (1984). *Qualitative data analysis: A sourcebook of new methods.* Beverly Hills, CA: Sage.

National Education Association. (1983). *The national teacher opinion poll* (Research memo). Washington, DC: Author.

National Education Association. (1990). *Estimates of school statistics.* West Haven, CT: Author.

Pfeffer, J. (1981). Management as symbolic action: The creation and maintenance of organizational paradigms. *Research in Organizational Behavior, 3,* 1-52.

Tesch, R. (1988, April). *The contribution of a qualitative method: Phenomenological research.* Paper presented at the annual meeting of the American Educational Research Association, New Orleans.

Resource B

RECOMMENDED BOOKS

Leadership

Barth, R. (1990). *Improving schools from within*. San Francisco: Jossey-Bass.

Blase, J., & Kirby, P. C. (1992). *Bringing out the best in teachers: What effective principals do*. Newbury Park, CA: Corwin.

Blumberg, A. (1989). *School administration as a craft: Foundations of practice*. Boston: Allyn & Bacon.

Bolman, L. G., & Deal, T. E. (1990). *Reframing organizations: Artistry, choice, and leadership*. San Francisco: Jossey-Bass.

Burns, J. M. (1978). *Leadership*. New York: Harper & Row.

Foster, W. (1986). *Paradigms and promises: New approaches to educational administration*. Buffalo, NY: Prometheus Books.

Gardner, J. W. (1989). *On leadership*. New York: Free Press.

Maxcy, S. J. (1991). *Educational leadership: A critical pragmatic perspective.* New York: Bergin & Garvey.

Parkay, F. W., & Hall, G. E. (1992). *Becoming a principal: The challenges of beginning leadership.* Needham Heights, MA: Allyn & Bacon.

Sergiovanni, T. J. (1991). *The principalship: A reflective practice perspective.* Boston: Allyn & Bacon.

Smyth, J. (1989). *Critical perspectives on educational leadership.* London: Falmer.

Teachers as Professionals

Shared Governance and Democratic Schooling

Dewey, J. (1916). *Democracy and education.* New York: Macmillan.

Dewey, J. (1938). *Experience and education.* New York: Macmillan.

Glickman, C. D. (1993). *Renewing America's schools: A guide for school-based action.* San Francisco: Jossey-Bass.

Glickman, C. D., & Allen, L. (Eds.). (1992). *The league of professional schools: Lessons from the field* (Vol. 1). Athens: University of Georgia, Program for School Improvement.

Glickman, C. D., & Allen, L. (Eds.). (1993). *The league of professional schools: Lessons from the field* (Vol. 2). Athens: University of Georgia, Program for School Improvement.

Teacher Empowerment

Kreisberg, S. (1992). *Transforming power: Domination, empowerment, and education.* Albany: State University of New York Press.

Maeroff, G. I. (1988). *The empowerment of teachers: Overcoming the crisis of confidence.* New York: Teachers College Press.

The Professionalization of Teaching

Firestone, W. A., & Bader, B. D. (1992). *Redesigning teaching: Professionalism or bureaucracy?* Albany: State University of New York Press.

Giroux, H. A. (1988). *Teachers as intellectuals: Towards a critical pedagogy of learning.* South Hadley, MA: Bergin & Garvey.

Gitlin, A., Bringhurst, K., Burns, M., Cooley, V., Myers, B., Price, K., Russel, R., & Tiess, P. (1992). *Teachers' voices for school change: An introduction to educative research.* New York: Teachers College Press.

Lieberman, A. (Ed.). (1988). *Building a professional culture in schools.* New York: Teachers College Press.

Schubert, W. H., & Ayers, W. C. (Eds.). (1992). *Teacher lore: Learning from our own experience.* New York: Longman.

Welker, R. (1992). *The teacher as expert: A theoretical and historical examination.* Albany: State University of New York Press.

Reflective Practice

Osterman, K. F., & Kottkamp, R. B. (1993). *Reflective practice for educators: Improving schooling through professional development.* Newbury Park, CA: Corwin.

Schön, D. A. (1983). *The reflective practitioner: How professionals think in action.* New York: Basic Books.

Schön, D. A. (1987). *Educating the reflective practitioner: Toward a new design for teaching and learning in the professions.* San Francisco: Jossey-Bass.

Schön, D. A. (Ed.). (1991). *The reflective turn: Case studies in and on educational practice.* New York: Teachers College Press.

Teaching

Teachers and Their Work

Connell, R. (1985). *Teachers' work.* Winchester, MA: Allen & Unwin.

Goodson, I. F. (1985). *Teachers' lives and careers.* London: Falmer.

Lortie, D. C. (1975). *Schoolteacher: A sociological study.* Chicago: University of Chicago Press.

Palonsky, S. B. (1986). *900 shows a year: A look at teaching from a teacher's side of the desk.* New York: Random House.

Reyes, P. (Ed.). (1990). *Teachers and their work place: Commitment, performance, and productivity.* Newbury Park, CA: Sage.

Rosenholtz, S. J. (1989). *Teachers' workplace: The social organization of schools.* New York: Longman.

Van Manen, M. (1986). *The tone of teaching.* Ontario, Canada: Scholastic-TAB Publications.

Philosophical Perspectives on Teaching

Greene, M. (1973). *Teacher as stranger.* New York: Wadsworth.

Noddings, N. (1984). *Caring.* Berkeley: University of California Press.

Rubin, L. J. (1984). *Artistry in teaching.* New York: Random House.

Tom, A. (1984). *Teaching as a moral craft.* New York: Longman.

Discourse and Narrative on Teaching

Ross, E. W., Cornett, J., & McCutcheon, G. (Eds.). (1992). *Teacher personal theorizing.* Albany: State University of New York Press.

Witherell, C., & Noddings, N. (Eds.). (1991). *Stories lives tell: Narrative and dialogue in education.* New York: Teachers College Press.

Values and the Ideology of Schooling

Apple, M. W. (1986). *Teachers and texts.* London: Routledge & Kegan Paul.

Grundy, S. (1987). *Curriculum: Product or praxis.* London: Falmer.

McNeil, L. (1986). *Contradictions of control: School structure and school knowledge.* New York: Routledge & Kegan Paul.

Memorable Teachers

Agers, W. (1989). *The good preschool teacher.* New York: Teachers College Press.

Epstein, J. (Ed.). (1981). *Masters: Portraits of great teachers.* New York: Basic Books.

MacCrorie, K. (1984). *20 teachers.* New York: Oxford University Press.

Group Development
and Interpersonal Communication

Johnson, D. W., & Johnson, F. P. (1987). *Joining together: Group theory and group skills.* Englewood Cliffs, NJ: Prentice Hall.
Luft, J. (1969). *Of human interaction: The Johari model.* Palo Alto, CA: Mayfield.
Schmuck, R. A., & Runkel, P. J. (1985). *The handbook of organization development in schools* (3rd ed.). Palo Alto, CA: Mayfield.

Index